To: _____

From: _____

ARMS OPEN WIDE

A CALL TO LINGER
in the SAVIOR'S PRESENCE

SHERRI GRAGG

THOMAS NELSON
Since 1798

NASHVILLE   DALLAS   MEXICO CITY   RIO DE JANEIRO

Published in Nashville, Tennessee, by Thomas Nelson. Thomas Nelson is a registered trademark of Thomas Nelson, Inc.

Cover design by Milkglass Creative.

Thomas Nelson titles may be purchased in bulk for educational, business, fund-raising, or sales promotional use. For information, please e-mail SpecialMarkets@ThomasNelson.com.

ISBN-13: 978-1-4003-2346-3

Printed in China

14 15 16 17 [TIMS] 5 4 3 2 1

www.thomasnelson.com

*I dedicate this book to Dr. Lucas Boyd, who
showed me the way . . . and told me I could.*

ACKNOWLEDGMENTS

———

WITH DEEPEST GRATITUDE TO the following:

My Messiah and Redeemer, Jesus Christ.

My large and beautiful family, who encouraged me and supported me every step of the way.

The good people at Thomas Nelson, for taking a chance on me, an unknown author. My publishing experience with you has been truly wonderful.

My brilliant editor, Lisa Stilwell. You are a gift from God.

The great men who have gone before me to study the sands where Jesus walked—Alfred Edersheim, Dr. James Martin, Kenneth Bailey, Ron Moseley, and so many more. As you opened my eyes to Middle Eastern life in the first century, the most amazing thing happened: God healed my heart. I am forever grateful.

CONTENTS

———

INTRODUCTION

———

ONE SUNDAY NIGHT LONG ago, I lay in bed as my heart pounded in my chest. Just that morning, a well-meaning Sunday school teacher had delivered a powerful lesson on the precarious state of my immortal soul without Jesus. I stared wide-eyed into the darkness for fear that if I closed my eyes and went to sleep I would awaken in eternal flames. Finally, when I could stand it no more, I slipped from beneath the covers and padded barefoot down the hall to my parent's room. My daddy and I sat on the side of the bed and I prayed to receive Christ as my Savior. I was four years old.

The infancy of my faith was founded not in Christ's tender love for me, but in the deep belief that He was a harsh judge who awaited the opportunity to throttle me. Throughout my childhood and youth, I kept this vengeful God at a distance and tried very hard to be good.

This flawed view of God and the fear that accompanied it would define my life for most of the next forty years. My misunderstanding of my heavenly Father stole my gifts. I was compelled to write from the time I was a child, but doubted myself too much to allow anyone to read my work. Close relationships were elusive for me because I was too busy hiding a heart I feared was unlovable. If my Creator was so displeased with me, how could anyone else accept me? The falsehoods I believed about God repeatedly drowned me in despair. Even on the days I knew the truth in my head, I struggled to untangle the tendrils of the lie from my heart.

It was not until I was forty-one years old and took a trip to Israel that I was introduced to the concept of interpreting scripture through the cultural lens in which it was written, and that the shackles on my heart and mind began to fall in earnest. Bit by bit, I learned to view Jesus' teachings through the eyes of a Middle Eastern Peasant. Scripture started to come to life for me. I found, at the center of humanity's tragic drama, a Messiah who was the incarnation of God Himself pouring out His life in costly love to redeem us all.

And I *loved* Him!

The writer of Hebrews says, "Jesus Christ is the same yesterday today and forever" (Hebrews 13:8.) In the spirit of this truth I have written each devotion with the hope of guiding you into His presence through fictional narrative surrounding Scripture. And while this is a creative work, it is one that is strongly rooted in research. For example, I do not know for certain that there was a narrow window near the ceiling of the room in which the sinful woman anointed Jesus' feet but I do know that this was the type of window commonly found in a first century home in Palestine. Also, some of the historical terms used may be unfamiliar to you. To address this, there is an asterisk after those words to indicate that a definition is provided in the glossary at the back of the book.

The prayers at the end of each chapter are very simply the cries of my own heart. However, I believe there are certain cries of the heart which are common to humanity. Maybe they'll even be a little like your heart's cry too.

My prayer for you while reading these pages is that you'll experience the same living and loving Savior as I have, and that you will truly know He stands with arms open wide to welcome you into His Father's kingdom just as you are.

Christ's peace,
Sherri

MASTER OF THE WIND AND THE WAVES

———

*Were you angry with the rivers, L*ORD*?*
Was your wrath against the streams?
Did you rage against the sea
when you rode your horses
and your chariots to victory?
You uncovered your bow,
you called for many arrows.
You split the earth with rivers;
the mountains saw you and writhed.
Torrents of water swept by;
the deep roared
and lifted its waves on high.

HABAKKUK 3:8–10

THE CROWDS WERE RELENTLESS. An endless sea of suffering humanity was tossed wave after wave upon the shore of Peter's doorstep—the feverish, the blind, the lame, the deaf, and, as evening drew near, the hordes of demon possessed. Jesus worked nonstop—touching them, speaking to them, freeing them, healing them.

And still they came, filling the courtyard and surrounding the house. No time to rest, no time to eat until, at last, the God-man could go no farther.

He held up a weary hand and motioned to His disciples to stem the flow of humanity coming through the door. He rose slowly, painfully, from the stool where He had been perched for hours and walked into the courtyard to survey the crowd. He would have to begin again tomorrow.

Jesus glanced back at Peter's home where He was staying and at the crowd that had no intention of leaving as long as He was present. He turned to His disciples and nodded toward the harbor.

"Let us go over to the other side" (Mark 4:35).

The men looked at each other warily. *"The other side?" Was the situation that desperate?*

The other side was local jargon for the opposite shore of the Sea of Galilee, the region of the Decapolis,* where observant Judaism* had been washed away by the tide of Hellenism. Amphitheaters and gymnasiums rose majestically next to the temples of Greek and Roman gods. It was a land where herds of pigs were raised—a practice the Jews considered abhorrent and unclean.

But Jesus began walking toward Capernaum's promenade and the pier where the disciples' boat was moored, so all that was left for them to do was follow. All along the way, the crowd pressed around Him, peppering Him with questions, begging for healing, and promising their allegiance.

Jesus and His disciples were leaving without even taking time to gather anything for dinner. It was going to be a long night.

The men began to prepare to launch the boat as Jesus settled down on the floor of the vessel near the stern. James pulled a heavy length of rope loose from the pier and began to roll it around his hand as he gazed out at the horizon where the sun was just beginning to set. He frowned and nudged John who turned to look in the same direction.

"Not one streak of red," James said.

"No," John said, frowning as he watched the sun sink below the horizon in a clear, pale blue sky. "We need to get moving. Just in case."

The other men glanced up at the sky and then at the Sea of Galilee, golden and silver in the waning light of the setting sun and the soft glory of the rising moon. A gentle breeze tugged at their robes as they shoved away from the pier. It was peaceful and beautiful, but they had been on the lake all their lives, and they knew just how quickly everything could change on a clear evening when the sky was gold instead of red.

Once in the open water, the disciples unfurled the sail. It flapped and then drew taut in the breeze. The men secured their oars and sat down to rest. Jesus sat with an elbow on the low wooden bench next to Him and gazed out at the peaceful lake. As the boat rocked gently back and forth, His eyes grew heavy, and, bit by bit, they began to close. He lay down onto the bench to rest His head on the cushion there. Soon He was asleep.

The other men slumped groggily against the sides of the boat, lulled by the steady breeze and the gentle rocking of the waves. Overhead, the moon rose high, turning the water silver with its light. One by one, stars began to pierce the night sky as warm air rose from the surface of the lake and began to collide with the cool air from the hills and plains that encircled its shores.

Suddenly, a fierce gust of wind rose from the east, caught the sail, and rocked the boat violently. The men shook themselves alert and scrambled for the oars as James and John began working to lower the sail and secure it to the mast. Another gust of wind ripped it from their hands. It began to flap wildly as they struggled to secure it again. Overhead, dark clouds began to roll and seethe, obscuring the moon and the stars. Jagged lightning ran along the undersides of the clouds, illuminating them from within. The lake, tranquil only moments before, answered the call of the gale. Their boat rose and fell as the water surged, molding into higher and higher waves and deep valleys. Soon the men were struggling against waves as high as six feet that tossed their vessel like a toy boat.

The men strained against the oars in an effort to keep the boat from capsizing. Peter was in the front nearest the bow, manning the steering oar. He pulled against his oar, willing it not to break as another wave slammed into the side of the boat and tossed a generous amount of water up over the side. He stared incredulously as white foam splashed onto the feet of Jesus, who somehow still managed to stay asleep!

The roar of the wind rose in its fury, as another wave, even larger than the last, crashed into the hull. This time, everyone received a lap full of water and several inches pooled in the bottom of the boat. A flash of lightning illuminated the churning sea as well as a fearsome landscape of gray mountains and dark valleys.

Peter's heart pounded in his chest. He tore his eyes away from the scene to look down at the water, ever rising in the boat, and then at Jesus asleep on the floor.

We are going down!

Peter shoved his oar aside and lunged toward Jesus, grabbing His leg and shaking Him awake as he shouted above the din of the storm.

"Teacher, don't you care if we drown?" (Mark 4:38). Grim faced, Peter sat back down to begin wrestling with the steering oar once again.

Jesus sat up and rubbed His eyes with the back of His hand. He took a long look at the terrified faces in front of Him and then at the raging sky above. He placed one hand on the edge of the boat and then pushed Himself to a standing position. Then He raised both arms above His head, His hands toward the heavens, and shouted.

"Quiet! Be still!" (Mark 4:39).

Immediately the wind died down to a gentle breeze and the sea grew calm. The clouds, which had been rolling above them only moments before, retreated, and a blanket of stars and a pale moon took their place above the water. Jesus sat back down in the bottom of the boat and turned to face His disciples who were sitting motionless but still gripping the oars. They stared at Him, pale with terror. *"Why are you so afraid?"* He asked. *"Do you still have no faith?"* (Mark 4:40).

The men looked at the clear sky above them and then back at the water still pooled around their ankles. They gazed at the surface of the lake, smooth as glass and silvery beneath the glow of the moon, and then at their own hands still dripping with water.

Numbly, the disciples bent forward, grasped the oars, and pulled. As Peter tugged at the steering oar to point the ship toward shore, a shocked voice from somewhere in the back expressed the thoughts in every heart.

"Who is this? Even the wind and the waves obey him!" (Mark 4:41).

Prayer

Oh, Master of the wind and the waves, be Lord over the storms in my heart. My faith, indeed, is small. Too often have I turned to You in my fear and asked, "Oh, Lord, don't You care?" And each time I've found You faithful. You are a good God, a caring Father. Help me to remember that I have nothing to fear because You love me and remain beside me in my ship of life.

Amen

BEAUTY FOR ASHES

For he will deliver the needy who cry out,
the afflicted who have no one to help.
He will take pity on the weak and the needy
and save the needy from death.

PSALM 72:12–13

Just that morning she had watched him in wonder as he prepared to leave for the fields. It seemed he had, by some mysterious spell, transformed from boy to man overnight. Each morning he seemed a bit taller than when he had gone to bed the evening before. She thought his changing body must be as strange to him as it was to her, for daily she watched him bump into stools, tables, and anything else that had the misfortune to be in his path.

He turned to pass through their doorway to meet his uncles and cousins who were in the courtyard preparing to leave for the day's work in the fields, and he knocked his forehead so hard on the door frame that it made an audible crack.

"Ouch!" he said, rubbing the quickly reddening patch just below his dark, wavy hairline.

She smiled, crossed the room, and brushed the spot gently with her fingertips.

Poor boy, she thought. *He is nothing but arms, legs, elbows, and knees—as awkward as a newborn calf.*

"My child," she chuckled, "you must be more careful with that head of yours. You may find yourself in need of it someday. Here, you almost forgot your wineskin."

"Thank you, Mother," he said. "I will see you in a little while."

Then he bent down to kiss her cheek good-bye, and she felt the soft brush of the first hints of his beard.

Her baby was becoming a man.

She stood in the doorway and watched him join the other men as they prepared to leave for the plowing. One of his uncles lay a large hand on his shoulder to whisper some secret instruction belonging to the world of men. For the thousandth time she breathed a prayer of thanks that God had provided her husband's brothers to guide her son carefully into manhood. After her husband's death, she never had to worry about who would train her young son to be a man; neither did she face the horror of finding a means for her own provision. Her only son earned her a position in the home of her husband's family. As long as he was living, she would have a roof over her head, protection, and food to eat. She knew not all widows were so fortunate.

In a moment she had finished tidying their living quarters and crossed the courtyard to join her sisters-in-law for the day's work. Today they would all be devoted to the hot, hard labor of dying the woolen yarn spun earlier in the week. When she arrived, she saw that one woman had already filled the large pot with water, so she began to get the fire started underneath it.

The morning sped by with their labors, and soon it was almost noon. She took her turn at the pot, stirring the yarn in the dye with a long wooden paddle. Sweat dripped down the side of her face and soaked the neck of her robe. The sun grew hot, and the lively conversation that had sweetened their labors in the morning stilled under the heat until the only sound was the dye lapping in the pot and the fire crackling beneath it.

Somewhere in the distance she heard shouting. The paddle stilled in her hands as she turned to listen. The shouting grew a little closer, and she dropped the paddle completely. Slowly, she walked a few steps toward the gate as the first tendrils of terror began to wrap around her heart.

Another shout, this time clearer and closer. She ran across the courtyard to the gate and saw the men approaching. They appeared to be carrying someone.

Somehow, she knew it was her son.

They drew nearer, and she saw the lanky arms and legs that had passed through her doorway so full of life just a short time ago, but now they were draped limply in the arms of his uncles. Large drops of blood splattered into the dust.

She cried out and ran to him. He was alert, but his face was deathly pale, and when he looked at her, his eyes were filled with a terror so profound that it washed away all traces of the man, leaving only her little boy behind.

"What happened?!" she cried as the men rushed across the courtyard toward the rooms she shared with her son.

"We were attempting to clear a large boulder from the south field. It shifted suddenly. He lost his footing, fell, and was partially pinned beneath it," one of the men said as they ducked into the cooler shadows of the room.

Quickly they laid him on his bed. She took his face in her hands and whispered a few brief words to comfort and calm him. Then she took a deep breath and evaluated his injuries. His left shoulder and arm were obviously crushed, but even with that he might survive. Her heart told her, however, that something far more menacing lay beneath the dark, wet spot on the front of his tunic. She clutched the top of the garment and ripped it in two to expose the wound.

What she saw made her lose all hope. The jagged edges of two broken ribs protruded from a gash in his side that oozed a steady stream of blood, already soaking the mat beneath him. Her sisters-in-law gasped and quickly began to gather strips of linen to stem the flow of blood. It was all they could do.

But it was not enough.

She knelt beside his bed to stroke his hair and
kiss his face, just as she had done while coaxing
him to sleep when he was a toddler.

"Mother . . ." he said just once. His breath became raspy, then shallow, and then not at all.

"Noooo . . ." she wailed. "No, no, no. . . ."

She climbed onto the bed, gathered him into her arms, rocked him, and wept.

Her husband's family stood around her in shock. Tears flowed down their faces, but no one spoke, for what words could be said to a widow who had just lost her only son?

As the sun began to cast long shadows across the room, she laid him gently on the bed before leaning over to kiss his forehead, right below the hairline where a new bruise was just beginning to form. Then she turned and walked to her room.

She stood in the doorway for a moment and rested her head wearily against the frame. Then she took a long, shuddering breath and crossed the room to open a basket she had last touched years before. A long, sacklike garment was inside. It was coarse and black, woven from goat hair. She unfolded and shook it. Ten-year-old ashes fell from the folds and scattered across the floor

She had last worn it for her husband. Now
she would wear it for their son.

She dressed in the garment, buried her face in her hands, and began to weep. Deep, agonizing sobs shook her frame as she twisted trembling fingers into her hair. Then as the crescendo of her wailing filled the air, she ripped a fist full of hair from her scalp and released it to the floor. She tore at her hair over and again, as long black tresses streaked with gray fell around her feet. When she finished she walked across the room to the oven, cupped her hands, and thrust them into the soft, cool ashes until her hands were filled. She then lifted her hands above her head, closed her eyes, and let the ashes fall onto her raw scalp, and down onto her shoulders.

Then she turned her face toward heaven and screamed.

When she returned to the courtyard, she found the familiar business of mourning underway. While she had been attending to the outward expressions of her loss, her family had begun making provisions for the burial. Tradition mandated that the dead be buried on the day of their passing, and there was much to be done. The women in her family had washed the body, anointed it with perfumed oils, and then wrapped it in white strips of linen lined with spices. The men had hired the professional mourners and a flutist and then secured the bier for transporting the body to the small cemetery on the hill just outside the city wall.

Women surrounded the heartbroken mother and wrapped her in supportive arms as the men carried her son's body into the street on the bier. When she walked outside, she found a huge crowd of neighbors, friends, and even strangers, silent and solemn in the face of her devastating loss.

As if on cue, the procession moved forward, the flutist began to play, and the mourners began to wail a high-pitched, unearthly cry.

She began to sob, her tears tracing ever widening paths through the ashes on her face. Strong arms led her through the streets and out the city gate, but she was unaware of anything except the bier in front of her and her own torrent of grief.

Then something cut through her darkness. It was a voice—powerful, yet gentle, and heavy with compassion—and it said to her the most inappropriate and unlikely thing imaginable.

"Don't cry" (Luke 7:13).

Don't cry? Who would say such a thing? If she cried without ceasing every moment for the rest of her life, it would never touch the depth of her loss!

Through the blur of her tears, she saw Jesus walk toward the bier and then lay His hand on it to halt its progress. The men carrying it stood still as the crowd settled into an uneasy silence. Then He turned and spoke directly to the corpse.

"Young man, I say to you, get up!" (Luke 7:14).

In immediate obedience to the command, there was a rustling of spices and cloth as long limbs struggled to free themselves from their linen bonds. The boy shook his head from side to side, and the linen cloth that covered his face fell from the bier and fluttered to the ground. Then the bewildered boy sat straight up. The pallor of death had been chased away by the ruddy glow of youth.

Jesus smiled, took his hand, helped him down, and then led him to his mother.

Death to life. A spirit of despair traded for a garment of praise.

Beauty for ashes . . .

Prayer

God of All Comfort,

There are moments in life that define our faith, days that make us question what we really believe. In those silent, midnight-dark hours of suffering, we discover what it means to bear hemorrhaging wounds of the soul, wounds that have no cure. Crushed by loss, we learn that hearts truly do break. Blinded by pain, we forget to breathe.

Meet me there, my God, or I will be consumed. Hold me near lest I lose all hope. Breathe on me, and I will live again.

Amen

THE UNTOUCHABLE ONE

On the day you were born your cord was not cut, nor were you washed with water to make you clean, nor were you rubbed with salt or wrapped in cloths. No one looked on you with pity or had compassion enough to do any of these things for you. Rather, you were thrown out into the open field, for on the day you were born you were despised.

Then I passed by and saw you kicking about in your blood, and as you lay there in your blood I said to you, "Live!"

EZEKIEL 16:4–6

BY THE WINDOW, SHE waits. Day after day, month after month, year after long year, she sits like a specter, invisible to the throngs of life passing by in the busy street just on the other side of her wall. She listens and watches, living vicariously through neighbors, relatives, and old friends who, one by one, have all but forgotten her completely.

She is the most hopeless of the hopeless. Impure. Unclean. Most certainly cursed by God for some secret sin.

She is condemned. She is the untouchable one.

Some mornings she awakens to the memory of that day, twelve years before, when she entered this room for her time of ritual impurity. She was so relieved to claim her monthly time of rest and renewal. How could she have known that her haven of respite would become her prison?

As she stares at the thatched ceiling, hot tears fill her eyes and then run down the sides of her face, soaking through her ebony hair and onto the sleeping mat beneath her. The sun rises, a rooster crows, and her sleepy village awakens, but she remains on her bed. Her weak heart pounds with the effort to push what precious little is left of her lifeblood. There is no need to rise with her neighbors to greet the day.

She hears the sound of sheep bleating as they are led past her window to market. The deep voices of shepherds erupt into laughter at some shared joke. A little farther away in the center of town, two boys play tag around the gnarled roots of an ancient sycamore fig tree. Their playful squeals drift into her room, past shopkeepers and donkeys laden with their wares. Then, close by her window, two gossiping women trudge along, the water sloshing in the full jars they carry on their shoulders. As they pass her home, they whisper in scandalous tones, speculating about what horrible sin she must have committed to have met such a fate.

Her heart sinks under the weight of their judgment. She wants to cry out and tell them she has searched her heart and memory for twelve long years looking for her offense. She has spent hours on her face before Jehovah, begging to be shown what evil lies within her so that she can confess and then be made whole again. But heaven is silent. Surely God has forgotten her.

At noon the streets grow quiet under the stifling midday sun. The air in her room becomes oppressive, and, despite her continual efforts to keep herself clean, the heat bakes her blood-soaked rags, filling the air with the stench of death. She struggles to her feet and stands trembling before the window. Sunlight glints off the brilliant blue of the Sea of Galilee. She draws a breath of fresh air and closes her eyes as a gentle breeze blows from the water, sweeping wisps of hair back from her ashen face.

Hearing fishermen call to one another as they repair their nets, she quickly lifts her headscarf to cover her hair. As she does, the faded blue sleeve of her tattered linen robe slips to her elbow. Self-consciously, she tugs at it to cover the ugly scars that crisscross the inside of her forearm, the only fruit to come from the countless bleedings administered by the best physicians in their efforts to free her from her malady.

She leans against the wall, the cool breeze washing over her as the wind carries snatches of the fishermen's conversation to her.

" . . . a Healer . . ."

" . . . Miracle Worker . . ."

" . . . coming here . . ."

She turns her head, straining to catch more of the story.

" . . . His name is Jesus . . ."

Moments later the midday quiet is suddenly broken by the distant rumble of shouting voices as a mass of humanity begins to course through the village streets. She watches as fishermen abandon their nets and run toward the crowd. Shopkeepers burst sleepy-eyed from their naps and into the glaring sunlight to investigate the commotion. Babies are startled awake and begin to cry as their mothers snatch them from their beds and run toward the excitement.

She watches breathlessly as an old man leads his blind and aged wife, and a father carries his lame son in his arms. They are all running, and they are running to this Man named Jesus.

Her face flushes and her pulse quickens as her most desperate hope pulsates through every cell of her being . . .

Maybe He could heal me too.

> *She looks toward the crowd and then at her door.*
> *She knows it would be scandalous, absolutely*
> *unacceptable, for her to cross that threshold.*

For a moment, she imagines herself pushing through the crowd, making everyone she touched unclean . . . to defile a Rabbi.

The crowd nears, and she can glimpse a Man in the center around whom all of the masses seem to orbit. She moves to the doorway of her room, bracing her hands against each side as she gazes across the courtyard to the outer gate that leads into the street.

The roar of the crowd swells, and with a prayer for forgiveness, she pulls her headscarf close and runs.

In a few steps, she makes it across the courtyard and into the street just as the mayhem reaches her house. Trembling and gasping for breath, she pushes her way into the crowd. The sudden press of humanity hits her like a shock after twelve years devoid of human touch, but her eyes never leave the Man at the epicenter of the chaos. Using every ounce of strength she has, she pushes and shoves. Still, her progress is painfully slow, and each time she feels she has almost reached Him, she is shoved back once again by the swell of the crowd. Still, she presses on.

There is no way she can speak to Him without her violation of the Law becoming all too apparent. *If I can only touch Him,* she reasons, *I could be healed, and no one would ever have to know.*

As she stumbles, she catches a glimpse of His white prayer shawl.

Roaring fills her ears, and her vision begins to narrow as she struggles to remain conscious. Then, straining, she stretches out her hand through the jostling bodies, and her fingers brush the blue fringe of the garment.

She gasps as pure power floods through her. Immediately, she feels the bleeding stop. Her vision clears as strength and vitality course through every muscle, every bone, each and every cell.

Suddenly, Jesus stops, and the crowd becomes silent. He begins to search the faces surrounding Him, and she hears Him speak to His disciples.

"*Who touched me?*" Jesus asks (Luke 8:45).

The disciples are incredulous. The crowds are pressing against Him on all sides. *Everyone* is touching Him.

But this touch was different, and Jesus knows it.

"*Someone touched me; I know that power has gone out from me*" (Luke 8:46).

She is terrified. Trembling, she begins to try to back out of the crowd, searching for somewhere, *anywhere,* to hide. Her face flushes with shame, and she pulls her headscarf closer.

The disciples are exasperated, but Jesus refuses to move. His eyes rove back and forth searching the crowd.

A small sob catches in her throat as she realizes that hiding is futile. Shaking violently, she begins to make her way to the front of the silent crowd where she falls face down at His feet.

There, weeping, she tells Him everything. She tells Him about the twelve long years she spent in suffering and isolation, about how she had spent all she had on countless doctors who only made her sicker.

She tells Him that, for all practical purposes, she was one who was dead, but when she touched Him, she was raised to life again.

A murmur of disapproval sweeps through the crowd as she trembles at His feet, awaiting this Rabbi's rage at having been defiled by her.

She braces herself for condemnation, but instead He stoops down in front of her.

"*Daughter,*" Jesus says with infinite gentleness. Slowly, she lifts her eyes to meet His. Where she expects to see anger, she finds only tender compassion.

"*Your faith has healed you. Go in peace*" (Luke 8:48).

Prayer

My Healer,

Thank You for seeing me in my need, inviting me to come to You, and waiting for me with arms open wide. Where others see scandal, You see my sorrow. When others have forgotten me, You remember me, and You know my grief. Even when my shame compels me to hide and fear cripples me, You stand immovable, ready to make me whole.

Grant me the faith to run after You with abandon, counting all else as loss. May my most desperate moments be the times when I discover You anew to be my Tender Savior, Wonderful Counselor, Mighty God.

Amen

"Follow Me"

The Call of Matthew

*"I will restore you to health and heal your wounds,"
declares the LORD, "because you are called
an outcast, Zion for whom no one cares."*

JEREMIAH 30:17

*For I desire mercy, not sacrifice, and acknowledgement
of God rather than burnt offerings.*

HOSEA 6:6

MATTHEW REACHED ABOVE HIS head to adjust the tarp over his customs booth to keep the sun out of his eyes. Then he settled back into his seat to watch as a crowd gathered around the Prophet from Nazareth. Soon Jesus began teaching them, and although Matthew pretended to review his accounts, he was intently listening to every word the Man from Galilee said.

Matthew had been observing Jesus for some time from his booth in Capernaum. Jesus frequently taught large crowds near the sea, and Matthew's customs booth gave him a front-row seat. He had seen Jesus heal the sick and cast out demons as well. Sometimes on the Sabbath, but not often, Matthew even slipped in the back of the synagogue to listen as Jesus taught. Matthew knew he wasn't exactly welcome there. According to rabbinical teachings, tax collectors, or publicans, were the most sinful of sinners.

And Matthew was the worst kind of publican. There were two basic categories. A *Gabbai,** (gab-bah'ee) was a despised general tax collector. But Matthew was a *Mokhes,** a customhouse official, and that position was even worse. While both groups reported to the Romans and were therefore considered traitors to their own people, *Mokhes* were especially despised for their seemingly endless opportunities for harassment and extortion. A *Mokhes* could charge all manner of taxes in addition to duties on imports and exports. There were bridge tolls, road tolls, and harbor dues too. There were possible taxes on wheels, pack animals, axles, and pedestrians. The list was as limitless as a *Mokhes'* imagination.

Furthermore, the *Mokhes* also had the authority to intercept travelers and require them to completely unload their pack animals for inspection down to the tiniest package and most personal scroll. Of course such inconveniences could be avoided . . . for a fee.

According to everything Matthew had ever learned about God, there was no hope for a *Mokhes* like him. Repentance meant turning oneself around, cleaning up, doing right. It meant making restitution above and beyond one's sin. As the rabbis said, "For herdsmen, tax collectors, and publicans is repentance hard."[1]

The path to God was just too steep for a tax collector. So Matthew had given up on the idea of ever becoming anything more than what he was. But then the Prophet from Nazareth came to town.

For a while, Matthew had enjoyed a front-row seat to Jesus' ministry and plenty of time to ponder quietly all he witnessed. The message Jesus preached about the kingdom of God was unlike any Matthew had ever heard. Jesus taught that God welcomed sinners no matter their past. Jesus spoke of forgiveness of sins, actual *forgiveness*. Jesus swept away the impossible path of repentance that His contemporaries had paved with good works, and he redefined it as a simple *willingness of the lost to be found*. This message was the antithesis of all Matthew had ever been taught about God.

And no one could deny Jesus' authority. He had healed a paralytic man right there in Capernaum. At this Rabbi's touch, the blind saw, the lame walked, and the mute spoke. Even the demons obeyed Him.

Day after day, month after month, Matthew watched and listened until, somewhere deep in his heart, a spark of faith ignited. If God were willing to receive him, Matthew was willing to be brought home.

But he still couldn't bring himself to approach Jesus. He was still a *Mokhes,* and the weight of public scorn was too heavy. So Matthew believed and hoped quietly from his customs booth, unsure of what to do next.

Matthew watched as Jesus finished teaching and then dismissed the crowd. A strong, steady breeze blew in from the Sea of Galilee, and white sails bobbed over the water against the backdrop of a flawless blue sky. Jesus stood and looked across the promenade at Matthew. The tax collector self-consciously averted his gaze and pretended to inspect his accounts again.

But Jesus had been watching Matthew, too, and He had seen the spark of faith in his heart. Jesus walked over to the customs booth, and the *Mokhes*, so hated by all, turned his eyes up to meet the Savior's.

"Follow me," Jesus said to him (Mark 2:14).

Matthew smiled. Then he stood and walked away from his booth, his accounts, his gold, his past—and into his new life. The other tax collectors noticed the interaction and followed the two men to Matthew's house. Matthew threw open his doors and spread the table with food and wine. Soon his home was crowded with *Mokhes* and *Gabbai*, tax collectors and sinners. Jesus sat in the middle of them all, laughing and enjoying the meal.

His presence with them demonstrated a powerful truth about the kingdom of God. In their culture, a meal was never simply a meal. To eat with someone communicated deep and sincere *acceptance* of that person.

Some local Pharisees heard of the spectacle and dropped in to investigate. Jesus was receiving these sinners? It was outrageous!

The Pharisees cornered some of Jesus' disciples to question His propriety.

"Why does he eat with tax collectors and sinners?" they demanded (Mark 2:16).

When Jesus lowered His goblet and turned to the Pharisees, the table grew silent.

"It is not the healthy who need a doctor, but the sick," He said to them. *"But go and learn what this means: 'I desire mercy, not sacrifice.' For I have not come to call the righteous, but sinners"* (Matthew 9:12–13).

Jesus turned from the Pharisees and back to the dinner conversation.

He had important work to do. He was welcoming sinners into the kingdom of God.

Prayer _____

Friend of Sinners,

Thank You for welcoming me to the Father just as I am. I am so glad to know my salvation does not hinge on my efforts or on my ability to make restitution for all I have done wrong. All I have to do is be willing to be found by You.

Amen

1. Babylonian Talmud, Baba kamma, 94b Barita

THE RESTORER
HAS COME

The Woman at the Well

"Come, all you who are thirsty,
    come to the waters;
and you who have no money,
    come, buy and eat!
Come, buy wine and milk
    without money and without cost.
Why spend money on what is not bread,
    and your labor on what does not satisfy?
Listen, listen to me, and eat what is good,
    and you will delight in the richest of fare."

ISAIAH 55:1–2

JUST BEFORE THE SIXTH hour, when the sun was high in the sky, she stepped across the threshold of her home and pulled the heavy wooden door closed behind her. She paused for a moment to secure her veil, roll up her leather bucket, and tuck an empty water jar into the crook of her arm. Then she took a few steps forward and peered cautiously into the street. Thankfully, it was deserted. All of her neighbors had wisely retired indoors to avoid the brutal midday sun.

She took a deep breath and walked toward the city gate. If she hurried, perhaps she could fill her jug and make it back home before the good citizens of Sychar stirred from their naps. Head down, she walked as quickly as she could past shops and row upon row of houses of the upright, respectable, and just. A noise to her right startled her, and she turned just in time to make eye contact with a woman tossing dirty water into the street. She felt her cheeks burn with familiar shame as the surprise registering in the woman's eyes quickly gave way to judgment and disgust.

So easy for her to judge, she thought. *What does she expect me to do? Live in a cave? Starve?*

A moment later she at last left Sychar behind. She slowed her pace a bit and turned onto the path to the well. The sun beat down onto the top of her head covering, and rivulets of sweat coursed down her scalp, neck, and back. Then she turned the corner, and the well was in sight.

But there was a Man sitting on the capstone of the well, and not just any man. Obviously a *Jewish* man. She paused at a distance, waiting for Him to notice her and move away—as custom dictated—so that she might come to the well to draw water. He turned in her direction and then away again, but He did not move.

She groaned in frustration. She looked at Him, back at Sychar (from where no help would come), and then at the empty jar in her arms. Water she needed, and water she would have! What was propriety to her anyway?

She took a deep breath, unfolded her bucket, and moved decisively to the well. She set her water jug against the base of the well before busily focusing her attention on positioning the two crisscrossed sticks in the mouth of the leather bucket to keep it open while it was being filled. Then she began to attach the rope.

He turned to her.

"Will you give me a drink?" He asked (John 4:7).

> *She was incredulous. "You are not only a Man,*
> *but a Jewish Man. I am a Samaritan woman,*
> *and You are asking me for a drink?*

"How is that going to work? Isn't everything about me, even my little bucket, a bit too defiled for You?"[1]

Jesus answered her, *"If you knew the gift of God and who it is that asks you for a drink, you would have asked him and he would have given you living water"* (John 4:10).

She leaned against the well and sighed in exasperation.

"Sir, You have nothing to draw with, and this well is deep. You can't even draw from here, much less get spring water. Are You greater than our father Jacob? By the way, he gave this well to *us*, to the Samaritans, not to the *Jews*. And Jacob himself drank from it. And his sons and his livestock did too."[1]

Jesus answered, *"Everyone who drinks this water will be thirsty again, but whoever drinks the water I give them will never thirst. Indeed, the water I give them will become in them a spring of water welling up to eternal life"* (John 4:13–14).

She thought for a moment of the women who passed by her window morning and evening on their way to the well, their happy companionship, the comfort and protection of their friendships. Then she thought of her own hot, lonely walks to the well day after day at noon, with no one to help her even lift the full and heavy jar to her head. She thought of the loneliness. She thought of the shame.

She laughed ruefully. "Sir, give me this water so that I won't get thirsty and have to keep coming here to draw water" (John 4:15).

Very quietly He answered her, and His words swept away all pretense in order to reveal the reason for her broken heart.

"Go, call your husband and come back" (John 4:16).

She stiffened, took a deep breath, blinked back tears, and began to lower the bucket into the depth of the well.

"I have no husband," she replied.

With great tenderness Jesus answered her, *"You are right when you say you have no husband. The fact is, you have had five husbands, and the man you now have is not your husband. What you have just said is quite true"* (John 4:17–18).

She tugged at the rope again and again until her leather bucket broke through the surface of the well, splashing water gently on the capstone. She leaned down and poured some of it into her jar.

"Sir," the woman said, "I can see that you are a prophet" (John 4:19).

She handed the bucket to Him so He could drink and seized the moment to change the subject.

She wiped away a tear with the back of her hand and motioned to Mount Gerizim in the distance. "Our ancestors worshiped on this mountain, but you Jews claim that the place where we must worship is in Jerusalem."

Embarrassed, she was simply attempting to deflect attention from her shame. It never seriously occurred to her that He would enter into a theological discussion, treating her as an equal, yet that is exactly what He did.

"Woman," Jesus replied, *"believe me, a time is coming when you will worship the Father neither on this mountain nor in Jerusalem. You Samaritans worship what you do not know; we worship what we do know, for salvation is*

from the Jews. Yet a time is coming and has now come when true worshipers will worship the Father in the Spirit and in truth, for they are the kind of worshipers the Father seeks. God is spirit, and his worshipers must worship in the Spirit and in truth" (John 4:21–24).

She stared at Mount Gerizim and pondered this Man's words. *Such complicated matters. Who could understand them?* Suddenly, she was overwhelmed with longing for the One the Samaritans called the Restorer, the Messiah. When He came, He would explain these things and make all things new. *Oh, how she needed Him to make all things new.*

With a deep sigh of longing, she said, "I know that Messiah" (called Christ) "is coming. When he comes, he will explain everything to us."

Then Jesus declared, "*I, the one speaking to you—I am he*" (John 4:25–26).

Just then there was a noise on the pathway behind her. She turned to find several more Jewish men approaching. A couple of them had loaves of bread in their hands.

His companions.

And they were obviously stunned to find Him speaking with her, a Samaritan woman. They approached cautiously and then stood silently, awkwardly to the side.

She turned from them and back to the Man sitting on the well. She looked into His face for a long moment.

How long had it been since someone had treated her with dignity? Kindness?

She, the one accustomed to being used and discarded? She, who was so familiar with scorn? She, who walked to the well alone in the heat of the day?

Restorer . . .

"*I who speak to you am He . . .*"

Without a word, she turned and ran toward Sychar, leaving her water jar at the well. When she burst through the gate, the city was awake again, the streets filled with her neighbors. She had to tell them—*convince them*—to come see this Man at the well, but how? What could she say to get them to listen?

Suddenly it occurred to her! She would need to use the only thing she had—her reputation.

She closed her eyes, took a deep breath, and stepped from the shadows of her past into the purpose of her future. With a loud voice, she called, "Come, see a man who told me everything I ever did. Could this be the Messiah?" (John 4:29).

All around her, activity ceased. Baskets and jars were lowered to the ground. Hands were wiped on aprons, and donkeys were tied to posts. Then they all followed her to the city gate. This time the entire town accompanied her on the path she had walked so many times alone. Messiah, the Restorer, had come.

Prayer

Restorer of All,

Thank You for looking past my guilt, my failures, and my shame to call forth in me all that is beautiful—for the glory of Your name. No matter how devastating my choices, You hold out hope for the promise of my future. You, my Gentle Redeemer, the Great I Am, make all things new. Restore me again.

Amen

1. Author's translation

The Faith of the Syro-Phoenician Woman

"I, the LORD, have called you in righteousness;
I will take hold of your hand.
I will keep you and will make you
to be a covenant for the people
and a light for the Gentiles,
to open the eyes that are blind, to
free the captives from prison
and to release from the dungeon
those who sit in darkness."

ISAIAH 42:6–7

She counted the coins carefully before placing them in the pouch that hung around her neck. Then she took her young daughter by the hand and stepped into the early morning sunlight.

"Are you ready for market, my flower?"

The little girl nodded her head enthusiastically. Big brown eyes fringed with long lashes crinkled as the child smiled up at her. The mother paused for a moment and bent down to lovingly brush long ebony ringlets from her face. She cupped the little girl's chin in her hand for a moment and scanned her face anxiously before placing a gentle kiss on her forehead.

"I love you, little one," she whispered.

"I love you, Mommy."

Mother and daughter began walking toward the center of town hand in hand. The main road of Zarephath was paved with large stones. The houses on either side of the road were close together, but as mother and daughter drew closer to the center of town, residences increasingly gave way to commerce. Metallurgists worked over glowing kilns. Sparks flew and hammers fell as the sound of their craft drifted through the village. Nearby, a potter sat in the sun painting a floral pattern on a bowl as delicate as an eggshell. His brush dipped over and again into red and then yellow as he created a work of art for some rich man's table. Soon, the pair neared the pride of Zarephath, the dyer's shop.

Folded lengths of luxurious purple cloth were stacked neatly for display on a table near the entrance. On a line nearby, still-wet fabric, dark as wine, rippled and danced in the steady ocean breeze. The dyer bent over his work. He held a rough sea snail, a murex,* in his hand. With expert precision, he pried open the shell and extracted a white vein from the snail. With steady hands he began to harvest a yellow fluid from the vein, letting it drip into a glass vial. As soon as the fluid came into contact with the air, it changed from yellow to a dark rose color. When this fluid was diluted, the result was the prized purple dye.

Suddenly, the little girl stopped walking. She abruptly turned her head hard to one side and began to moan and cry. She wrenched her hand from her mother's and began pacing back and forth as she mumbled and then laughed to herself. As suddenly as the frantic pacing began, it stilled. She stood frozen for a moment, and then she slowly turned toward the dyer's shop.

For the mother, time seemed to stop as every detail about the moment came into crisp focus—the fishy smell of the dye as it sloshed gently against the glass vial, the sound of a thousand crushed murex shells crunching beneath the child's sandals as she began to run, and then the little girl's small hand grasping the vial of precious liquid with unnatural suddenness.

The dyer was shocked for a moment, but then he roared his anger and grasped for the vial. The child stepped deftly out of his reach and then dangled the fragile container aloft and at arm's length. Without uttering a word, she had clearly communicated her threat.

The red-faced dyer took a deep breath and stepped back. His jaw was set and his nostrils flared in fury, but he did not risk moving or speaking. He stood perfectly still, keeping one wary eye on the child while watching as her mother quietly approached her from behind.

The mother held her breath. Her eyes were fixed on the expensive dye in her child's hand. The murex shells being crunched underfoot seemed as loud as the waves crashing on the shore. Beads of sweat gathered on her forehead as she neared the little girl. Then, just as she reached around her from behind to grasp the vial, the child smiled and released her grip.

The delicate glass jostled for a moment between their hands, and the rose-colored dye sloshed up the sides. By some miracle, the woman caught and secured the vial in her trembling palm. She took a deep breath and carefully handed it back to its owner. He began threatening her, shouting his condemnation and wrath, but she didn't hear, for as soon as the vial was secure, the child became filled with rage.

The mother picked her up and attempted to leave the shop with her, but the little girl now possessed an unearthly strength. Her small fists rained down on her mother. The child screamed and dragged her fingernails across her mother's face, drawing blood. Once they were in the street, the entire town stopped to watch the struggle. Looking around for somewhere to get the child out of sight, the mother spotted an alleyway that led behind the dyer's shop and to the shore.

Weeping, she picked up the raging child, soothing her through her tears. "My flower, my flower . . ."

Suddenly, the child stopped still, drew back in her mother's arms, and looked directly into her face. But it was not her little girl peering out from behind the eyes.

"Your flower?" A guttural voice sneered. "Your flower isn't here . . ."

The mother began to sob, begging for her child. "Please, please leave my baby. What do you want from me?"

A deep, menacing laugh of pure evil shook the child. Her eyes rolled back in her head, and she screamed before collapsing unconscious in her mother's arms. The weary mother sat down against a nearby wall next to the dyer's pools of murex. She turned her face to the sea and closed her eyes. The gentle ocean breeze blew her hair back from her face as she took deep, shuddering breaths in an attempt to calm her soul.

A few moments later, the child sleepily lifted her head. She stared at her mother for a moment before gently lifting a small hand to pat at the tears on her mother's face. She frowned and tenderly touched the bloody red welts on the woman's cheeks.

"Mommy," she asked groggily, "what happened to your face?"

"Oh, it's nothing," she responded with an exhausted half-smile.

The child looked down and spotted the snail pools. She scrambled from her mother's lap to lie weakly by the pools and peer into the depths. She reached out and gently trailed one small finger across the surface of the water.

A little while later, after they returned home and the child lay napping in her bed, the mother began working in the kitchen. The dough moved expertly in her strong hands, but her thoughts were far from her kneading bowl. As she had passed through the market on her way home, she had heard that Jesus of Nazareth was in town. His fame had spread throughout the entire region because of the mighty miracles He performed. Some of the Jews even whispered that He was the Son of David, the Messiah. This was not His first trip to the region. He had previously visited nearby Tyre and Sidon. She heard He was not only mighty but that He offered compassion to all, Jew and Gentile alike. Most Jewish men would never even speak to a Gentile, certainly not a Gentile woman, but this Man was rumored to be different.

At that moment, the child began moaning in her sleep. The mother closed her eyes, took a deep breath, and wearily pulled her hands from the dough. She wiped them on the towel tied at her waist as her little girl now began to scream. Turning to kneel beside the child's bed, she saw that her little girl's body was rigid. Her chest rose and fell rapidly, and her face was purple.

Staring at her precious daughter for a moment, the mother then knew exactly what she had to do. She needed help.

She needed Someone not only stronger than the demon but Someone who was willing to help her.

She could think of only one Person.

She bent to kiss her daughter gently on the forehead and whisper a silent prayer for her protection.

She went to the door and took one last look back at her daughter before pulling it closed. Then she began running toward the center of town.

It didn't take long to find Him. She simply looked for the crowd.

She began weaving her way in and out of people, pushing past the unyielding and ignoring their dirty looks. When Jesus was in sight, she began calling out to Him, combining His messianic title with the cry of a beggar.

"Lord, Son of David, have mercy on me! My daughter is demon-possessed and suffering terribly" (Matthew 15:22).

He turned to the sound of her voice, and when His eyes met hers, she saw deep compassion there. His disciples, however, stared back at her in obvious disgust. They considered her—a woman and a Gentile—defiled, unclean, and unworthy of their time. Jesus turned from her and looked at His disciples. For the briefest of moments, she saw irritation register on His face and then determination. He looked her way once more and then turned away.

She moved closer. "Lord, Son of David, have mercy on me!" she pleaded.

The disciples turned to Jesus. "Send her away, for she keeps crying out after us" (Matthew 15:22–23).

Jesus looked deep into the woman's eyes and entrusted to her a great test. *"I was sent only to the lost sheep of Israel,"* He remarked (Matthew 15:24).

A tense silence fell over the crowd as her eyes searched His face. *Could it be?* No, she didn't believe it. She didn't believe He would turn her away so coldly.

She dropped to her knees before Him and, as tears streamed down her face, uttered the purest cry of her desperate soul.

"Lord, help me!" (Matthew 15:25).

Compassion flickered in His eyes as He saw the full depth of her anguish. Then He made a decision: to lay it bare for all to see. He knew that at the core of her wound lay a gem of courage and faith that would at last begin to uproot from His disciples, the future leaders of the church, the deeply embedded sin of prejudice. He would use her heart-wrenching situation to expose their prejudicial attitudes: their sin would be clearly revealed by the bright light of her suffering and faith.

"It is not right to take the children's bread and toss it to the dogs," He replied (Matthew 15:26).

She could have responded angrily to such a callous insult, but she didn't. She pressed on in the belief that Jesus was not only mighty enough to help her, but willing as well. She believed with all her heart that this Jewish Rabbi was different from the rest.

Once more, the stillness of expectation settled over the crowd as her eyes remained locked on the eyes of Jesus.

"Yes, Lord," she said, "yet even the dogs eat the crumbs that fall from their masters' table" (Matthew 15:27 RSV).

Jesus smiled down at her and shook His head. She had passed the most difficult of tests and, in the process, helped Him teach His disciples a powerful lesson.

"O woman," He said, *"great is your faith! Be it done for you as you desire"* (Matthew 15:28 RSV).

Prayer

Son of David,

Have mercy on me! When I am exhausted, brokenhearted, and worn thin by fear, have mercy on me. Help me remember that the most difficult tests You give me are not cruelties, but honors. Grant me the grace in those moments to cling to what I know to be true . . . and to await Your deliverance in quiet confidence and perfect peace.

Amen

THE LIGHT
OF THE WORLD

———

"Arise, shine, for your light has come,
and the glory of the LORD *rises upon you.*
See, darkness covers the earth
and thick darkness is over the peoples,
but the LORD *rises upon you*
and his glory appears over you.
Nations will come to your light,
and kings to the brightness of your dawn."

ISAIAH 60:1–3

THE MULTITUDE OF WORSHIPPERS filled the temple courts on the first night of the Feast of Tabernacles.* The oil lamps in their niches did little to banish the darkness in so vast a space. Men, women, and children jostled against one another as the priests took their positions for the final ceremony, the Joy of the Feast.*

Earlier in the evening, young men of priestly descent had climbed ladders to reach the top of the four enormous candelabras in the Court of Women.* Each attendant had carried a large pitcher of oil that he carefully used to fill the golden bowls at the top of the structures.

Now the priests began singing hymns, and a hush fell over the crowd as the attendants once again began ascending the ladders to the top of the candelabras, this time with torches in their hands. Every eye was trained upward in the darkness, and as the people waited for the light, they remembered the significance of the ceremony.

Light represented both the pillar of fire that had led their fathers in the wilderness as well as God's *shekhinah* glory.* The rabbis taught that God wrapped Himself in light as a garment that could not shine by day lest it dim the sun. His divine light was that from which the sun, moon, and stars had been kindled, and it was now reserved under the throne of God for Messiah when He came.

The light was representative of Messiah Himself too. He was the "great light" shining in the darkness (Isaiah 9:2) that God had promised to one day kindle for His people Israel.

When the attendants reached the top of their ladders, a holy silence fell over the crowd. Then slowly, in unison, these young men lowered their torches to the golden bowls. A roar of flame and wave of heat swept over the people as the temple courts were flooded with brilliant light. The people raised their voices in both gratitude for God's past deliverance and joyful expectation of the coming Messiah.

A few days later, Jesus of Nazareth stood in the temple courts and raised His voice:

"I am the light of the world. Whoever follows me will never walk in darkness, but will have the light of life" (John 8:12).

No one missed the significance of Jesus' statement, especially the temple leaders. Their distaste for the Prophet from Nazareth was developing into a murderous hatred.

The next Sabbath, as Jesus and His disciples were going to the temple, they walked past the many beggars waiting near the gates. On any other day, the unfortunate souls would cry out for alms, but it was against the law to beg on the Sabbath. One man, blind from birth, maintained his place on his mat in hopes that his mere presence might stir compassion in the heart of a few worshippers, and discreet gifts would follow. He sat cross-legged with his eyes closed and head down. One hand rested on his knee, and the other grasped a long stick he used to guide himself through Jerusalem's streets.

As they neared the man, the disciples saw a familiar expression of compassion on Jesus' face.

"Rabbi, who sinned, this man or his parents, that he was born blind?" they asked (John 9:2).

The disciples had been taught all their lives that physical deformities were God's punishment for sin. But what about a man who had been born blind? Who had sinned then? Was the man's father or mother to blame, or did he somehow sin while in the womb?

Jesus stopped in front of the beggar and knelt down before him. He reached out and placed a gentle hand on his shoulder.

"Neither this man nor his parents sinned," said Jesus, *"but this happened so that the works of God might be displayed in him. As long as it is*

day, we must do the works of him who sent me. Night is coming, when no one can work. While I am in the world, I am the light of the world" (John 9:3–5).

Jesus was redefining all that His disciples thought they understood about suffering and the nature of their fallen world. Jesus was explaining to them that creation was broken by sin and that suffering would inevitably follow as a result. Jesus was also holding out a new hope to them: having come as a light into the darkness, He had the power to *redeem suffering for the glory of God.* It was a promise true not only for the blind beggar, but for all who are wounded by the fall.

By this time, Jesus had the blind man's rapt attention. Jesus spat on the ground and began to knead the dirt between His fingers to make a small bit of mud. The disciples had seen spittle used for eye maladies many times. Although no one expected it to cure blindness, it was a common treatment. Jesus' actions would not have been considered terribly remarkable on any other day, but this was the Sabbath. The Jews' oral tradition forbade the application of *any* treatment of an illness on the Sabbath unless internal organs were threatened, but even then treatment was allowed only under the direst circumstances. And while it was acceptable to apply wine to the eyelid because wine qualified as a cleanser, applying it to the inside of the eye was unlawful. The application of saliva on the Sabbath was, in fact, expressly forbidden.

Jesus took the mud and put it on the man's eyes.

"Go," He told him, *"wash in the Pool of Siloam"* (John 9:7).

Then Jesus and His disciples proceeded into the temple.

The blind man's pulse was racing. He had heard about this prophet from Nazareth and the mighty works He had done. Could he dare hope that when He washed the mud from his eyes, he would be healed?

He stood to his feet and held his walking stick out in front of him, tapping it from side to side to feel for obstacles in his way. He knew the streets of Jerusalem well and had been to the Pool of Siloam many times. It was a very popular place.

A short time later he heard splashing and the voices of the other people at the pool. The blind man carefully walked up the short flight of stairs at the entrance of the pool and then stretched his stick in front of him to find a clear path to the water. After a few steps he felt his stick slip from the solid surface of the stone-paved platform to the water below. He had arrived. Trembling, he knelt on the stone and laid his walking stick to the side. Then he felt his way down the steps which framed the interior edge of the pool to ease into the water. He dipped his hands beneath the cool surface of Siloam, splashed the water over his eyes, and rubbed away the mud.

Brilliant, piercing light flooded his senses as his own hands came into focus. Next, he saw the sunlight dancing across the surface of the pool. He laughed and turned to see blues, purples, browns, and reds in the robes of the people around him. The verdant green of palm trees above his head swayed in the breeze, and beyond them stretched an endless blue sky.

Laughing again, he stood to his feet and shouted for all to hear.
"I can see! I can see! I can see!"

His walk home was awash in countless awe-inspiring images, but the wonder he felt was equaled by that of his neighbors upon seeing him for the first time after his healing. They had known him, defined him by his blindness, all of his life. Some of them struggled to believe the miracle standing before them.

"Isn't this the same man who used to sit and beg?" some of them asked (John 9:8).

"No," others said, "he only looks like him."

But he himself insisted, "I am the man."

"How then were your eyes opened?" they asked.

He replied, "The man they call Jesus made some mud and put it on my eyes. He told me to go to Siloam and wash. So I went and washed, and then I could see."

"Where is this man?" they asked him.

"I don't know," he said (John 9:8–12).

Ultimately, it was decided that an occurrence so astonishing should be brought before the Pharisees for investigation, so the crowd took the once-blind man to meet with them.

When the Pharisees repeated the same questions his neighbors had asked, the man patiently repeated his answers. Surely, the leaders of Israel would be in awe of such a miracle and rejoice that God was moving so powerfully in Jerusalem. But that was hardly their reaction. They couldn't get past the fact that Jesus had broken the Sabbath when He healed the man. It was impossible for them to conceive that Jesus could be from God if He did not keep the Sabbath according to *their* guidelines.

Searching for an answer to their quandary, they found a possible solution. Perhaps the man was lying about being born blind. The Pharisees decided to call his parents in for questioning and expose his deceit.

But his parents were afraid to be drawn into the discussion. They did not want to risk angering the Pharisees. They confirmed that the man was their son and that he had been born blind. All other questions would need to be answered by the man himself. They would have no part of it.

The tension in the room was building. The man knew what had happened to him and could not deny it. The Pharisees could not accept his account because it conflicted with their own misconceptions about God.

"Give glory to God by telling the truth," they said. "We know this man [Jesus] is a sinner."

*The man responded in frustration. "Whether
he is a sinner or not, I don't know. One thing
I do know. I was blind but now I see!"*

Then they asked him, "What did he do to you? How did he open your eyes?"

"I have told you already and you did not listen. Why do you want to hear it again? Do you want to become his disciples too?" he asked (John 9:24–27).

This response was more than the Pharisees could take. They were furious.

"You are this fellow's disciple!" they accused him. "We are disciples of Moses! We know that God spoke to Moses, but as for this fellow, we don't even know where he comes from."

The man laughed softly before responding. "Now that is remarkable! You don't know where he comes from, yet he opened my eyes" (John 9:28–30).

He paused for a moment before making his argument. "We know that God does not listen to sinners. He listens to the godly person who does his will. Nobody has ever heard of opening the eyes of a man born blind. If this man were not from God, he could do nothing" (John 9:31–33).

The leader of the Pharisees sneered at him. "You were blind from birth and you, who were marked as a sinner from the womb, dare to lecture us! You aren't worth any more of our time. Get out!"

The man sat outside the synagogue unsure what to do next. He knew he had told the truth. He also knew he could not possibly deny the One who had given him his sight.

A short time later a Man approached him and sat down beside him. When He spoke, His voice was familiar.

"Do you believe in the Son of Man?" Jesus asked him (John 9:35).

The man turned to Him. "Who is he, sir?" he asked Jesus with all the conviction in his heart. "Tell me who he is so that I can believe in him!"

Then Jesus honored his courageous faith and loyalty by offering the man who had been cast out of the synagogue a new home for his heart.

"You have now seen him; in fact, he is the one speaking with you" (John 9:37).

"Lord, I believe," the man said as he knelt before Jesus to worship Him.

Jesus said, *"For judgment I have come into this world, so that the blind will see and those who see will become blind."*

Some Pharisees who were standing nearby overheard Him. They laughed mockingly. "What? Are we blind too?"

Jesus said, *"If you were blind, you would not be guilty of sin; but now that you claim you can see, your guilt remains"* (John 9:39–41).

Prayer

Light of the World,

Your broken creation, marred by the fall, is full of trouble. Someday You will come and make all things new, but until that day there will be times when the road before me is marked with pain and suffering, accusations and judgment. What joy it brings my soul to know that my suffering need not be in vain because of Your cross. If I am willing to surrender my hurt to Your healing touch, You will bring it for the glory of God. There could be no sweeter promise for me, Your child.

I love You, Light of the World. Forever shine in me.

Amen

A KINGDOM FOR ALL

The Feeding of the 4,000

You will have plenty to eat, until you are full,
and you will praise the name of the Lord your God,
who has worked wonders for you.

JOEL 2:26

My house will be called
a house of prayer for all nations.

ISAIAH 56:7

Before you begin, read Matthew 15:29–38

I was thirteen and man enough to be off on an adventure with my friends, yet still boy enough for my mother to pack food for my journey.

"Be careful, my son," she said as she placed a tied cloth in my hands. I could feel the brittle outline of a couple of dried sardines and the warmth of fresh bread.

"Hurry, Aelius!" Marcus shouted to me from the street. "They say He is healing people on the mountainside. Crowds are coming from everywhere."

"I'm coming," I called to him before turning to my mother.

"I will be careful, Mother. See you in a couple days."

Then I was out the door to join my friends. We bolted down the street past merchants with their carts and the homes of our neighbors. We were headed toward the *Decumanus Maximus*,* the main street of Hippos, that stretched straight through the center of the city from the East Gate to the West. The street was bordered by hundreds of huge columns, each fifteen feet tall. All other streets in Hippos ran out from this main thoroughfare at right angles.

The *Decumanus Maximus* was in sight when we almost ran full tilt into a large hairy man as he exited the bathhouse. He growled at us, and we mumbled an apology. As he turned to leave, Luke motioned for us all to look into the door of the bathhouse he left ajar.

"Look at that!" he said, awestruck.

There, on the wall of the entrance hall, was a huge relief of Hercules.* He towered larger than life and in full color with a cape made from a lion's skin draped across his muscular back and a club in his hand. His hair and beard were long and wild. His face was filled with fury.

"Come on! Let's go," Marcus said, and we were off again. We took a left on the main street and darted past temples and fountains, and underneath shaded colonnades; our leather sandals pounded the stones beneath our feet.

We ran past the statue of the emperor, the guard tower, and through the western gate. At last, we began to make our way along the steep path that snaked down the side of the mountain as the sea glittered in the sunlight in front of us.

Marcus reached out a hand to stop us for a moment. We all caught sight of the crowds of people making their way from all directions to a small group of men on the mountainside.

It was the Healer.

Months before, the same mighty Man of God had come across the sea and cast the devils from the wild man who lived in the tombs—a man so violent that the strongest men in the Decapolis had attempted to bind him with chains to no avail.

Afterward, this man who had terrified the entire region went city to city bearing witness that the Man of God had freed him by simply speaking the words.

Now the Healer had returned, and people from all over the Decapolis were bringing their sick and disabled to Him in the hope that He might heal them.

We made our way down the winding path past the magnificent mausoleums of the city's elite, resplendent columned homes for the dead, to the foot of the mountain below. Once on level ground, we pushed our way through the crowd to climb a tree near the center of the action. We had perfect front-row seats. The Healer and His friends stood below us and a few feet to the left. Spread out before us in a great mass of humanity were the blind, deaf, and lame.

I watched breathlessly as an aged woman led her deaf and mute son to the Healer. He reached out and put His fingers in the young man's ears. The Healer closed His eyes and sighed before placing His fingers on the man's lips.

Suddenly, the young man's eyes grew wide as he turned toward his mother's voice. Then he laughed aloud and was startled by the sound of his own laughter. Jesus smiled in response to their thanks and then turned to the long line of suffering before Him.

We watched Him heal throughout the day. The blind left His presence seeing. The lame walked, and crooked limbs were made straight at the touch of His hand. As the sun set that evening, we ate from the provisions we had brought with us and settled down with the crowd to sleep under the stars for the night.

Camp began to stir the next morning with the first rays of sunlight as sleepy travelers rummaged through their belongings for their breakfasts. I sat up, rubbed my eyes, and untied my cloth to retrieve the last piece of my bread before shaking the crumbs onto the ground below. Soon, the Healer resumed His place. The line formed before Him, and He began His work once again. My friends and I climbed the tree to watch.

All that day and the next, people came. He touched each one, met each need.

Often our empty stomachs reminded us we
should start for home, but we could not bear
to leave the wonder of the next miracle.

Finally, at the end of the third day, the Healer looked about and found there was no one left to heal.

He surveyed the crowd before Him for a moment and then turned to His friends.

"I have compassion for these people; they have already been with me three days and have nothing to eat. I do not want to send them away hungry, or they may collapse on the way" (Matthew 15:32).

His friends turned to look at the crowd of more than four thousand before them and then back to Jesus.

"Where could we get enough bread in this remote place to feed such a crowd?"

"How many loaves do you have?" Jesus asked (Matthew 15:33–34).

They took a moment to confer with one another about the matter and then turned back to Him.

"Seven," they replied, "and a few small fish" (Matthew 15:34).

Jesus told the crowd to sit down on the ground. Then He took the seven loaves of bread and the few dried sardines in His hands and thanked God for them before breaking off pieces and handing them to His disciples to pass out to the people. When the men came to us in the tree, we took the food and gratefully ate our fill.

Seven small loaves, a few sardines, yet somehow the pieces kept coming until everyone was satisfied.

Jesus called for His friends to find baskets to pass around to collect the leftovers. Once they were finished, there were seven baskets full in all—far more food than what they had in the beginning. As the disciples brought the food to show Jesus, He explained to them that just as He had provided miraculously for five thousand Jewish pilgrims on the way to Passover not long before, He had now provided for us, the Gentiles of the Decapolis. He wanted them to know that the kingdom of God wasn't just for the Jews, that it had come for *all*.

I saw the man who had once lived in the tombs, violent and filled with demons, sitting nearby. Now he was peaceful and whole. I thought of mighty Hercules, slayer of lions, terrible in his wrath. Hercules either had been unwilling or unable to help that man.

I looked down at the baskets filled with bread and then to the crowd as they quietly made their way home—the blind seeing, the lame walking, the deaf hearing. None of my gods had ever done anything so great.

I dropped from the branches of the tree, hit the ground, and ran straight for Hippos.

"What's the rush?" Marcus yelled after me.

"I have to go tell my family!" I shouted back over my shoulder.

The kingdom of God had come for all . . .

Prayer _____

Healer,

> *You came for me when I was too helpless and blind to even know I needed You. You gave me eyes to see and ears to hear. You set me free and restored my soul. Thank You for extending the kingdom of God to me. In You I "live and move and have [my] being."[1] Let me never take for granted such amazing grace . . . offered to me, one who was so far away.*
>
> *Amen*

1. Acts 17:28

Forgiven

———

A bruised reed he will not break,
and a smoldering wick he will not snuff out.
In faithfulness he will bring forth justice.

Isaiah 42:3

THE SERVANTS BUSTLED AROUND the triclinium table* filling goblets with wine and piling platters high with olives, figs, and dates. A short, balding man rushed in from the kitchen. He reached up with a towel in his left hand to dab the sweat from his flushed face as he used his right arm to balance a tray of steaming lamb on his expansive belly. He surveyed the table for a moment before snarling in disgust.

"Bread! Bread!" he shouted over his shoulder. "Where is the bread?"

A wiry man whose dark beard was liberally flecked with gray walked quickly but calmly into the room cradling a large loaf of bread in his arms.

"Calm yourself, Matthias," he said. "It is right here." He placed the bread carefully in the center of the table before snapping his fingers at the other servants and motioning them each to their proper stations.

A young boy struggled to set a large jar of water near the door before placing a basin, towel, and small container of olive oil beside it for the customary washing and anointing of the guests' feet. He then rushed to straighten the stools around the table where the guests would rest while the servants completed their tasks. At last, he joined the other servants as they retired to their posts. Bit by bit the room grew silent in anticipation of the imminent arrival of the master of the house and his guests.

Sunlight streamed into the room from the narrow windows near the ceiling, illuminating countless dust particles floating in the air. The beams of light fell across the banquet table, the robes of the servants, and finally upon the silent row of outcasts seated on the floor along the wall. Remarkably, these—the rejected and unclean—had been welcomed into Simon the Pharisee's home. When he fed them at the end of the banquet, he would demonstrate his generosity and nobility for all to see. Their need and shame were an important part of any feast hosted by a wealthy and well-respected man.

Among these props in this righteous man's production of holiness was a mere sinful woman. She had come as an outcast to the house of a Pharisee not to be fed, but to pour out her heart in gratitude. She could still hardly believe the message she had heard young Rabbi Jesus preach on the temple steps. He spoke not of some new interpretation of the Sabbath or of God's coming judgment for His sinful, wayward people. Instead, He said God loved His children—even the sinful ones—and would stop at nothing to bring them close to Himself. According to Jesus, God would search for sinners as a shepherd searches for a lost sheep or a woman might search for a precious lost coin. She had heard many rabbis speak, but most of them did so with angry scowls and pointing fingers.

This Man spoke with kindness and forgiveness, and His words reverberated deep within her soul until she believed that His message of forgiveness was for her too.

She desperately wanted to express her thanks to Him, so when she heard He would be dining at Simon's house for examination by the older rabbis, she had seized the opportunity to express her thanks to the One who had set her free.

Her reflections and the stillness of the moment were broken by Simon as he strode commandingly into the room. He surveyed the setting with approval before bending to speak in hushed tones to Matthias. The servant seemed confused for a moment, but the confusion quickly gave way to shock as his face reddened and he nodded in quiet assent. At that moment, the approaching guests could be heard chatting in the courtyard, and Simon turned and smiled broadly at the door. As each man entered, the host spoke a warm greeting and kissed him on the cheek before motioning him to the stools where a servant waited to wash and anoint his feet.

The woman clasped a smooth, cold alabaster jar of costly perfume beneath the folds of her robe as these rituals were performed. Her heart pounded as she watched each face cross the threshold. Once Jesus entered and Simon greeted Him, He would then move to the stool for the servant to wash His feet. At that moment, she would approach and anoint His hands and head with the perfume.

At last, Rabbi Jesus arrived. She shifted her weight to rise as He moved toward Simon to receive His greeting, but instead of greeting Jesus with a kiss, Simon reached past Jesus to the man behind Him. A series of quiet, shocked gasps echoed along the row of outcasts as they witnessed the snub. She grasped the alabaster jar tighter as she watched Jesus bow His head for a moment and then move to the line of men awaiting the attendance of the servants. Matthias flushed a deeper red, then looked past Jesus and motioned the servants to care for each and every man present except Him. Jesus waited quietly for a moment and then moved purposefully to the head of the table and reclined, His feet unwashed.

As she watched His humiliation, her vision blurred with tears that first streamed down her face and then dripped onto the front of her robe. This Man, who had spoken words of life and freedom to her, had been invited to the banquet as a guest and then purposefully shunned. What was more, now that He was reclining at the triclinium table, his head and hands were far away from her at the center of the structure. It would be socially impossible for her to anoint His hands and head as she had planned. She sat watching as Simon and the others laughed and talked.

Jesus might have been at the table, but He was an outcast just like her.

It was more than she could bear. She no longer cared what consequences would come her way—whether it be shame, or beatings, or being cast into the street. She stood to her feet as the eyes of the other outcasts turned to her in horror. Slowly, tears still flowing, she made her way across the room. The servants were moving about, and at first no one at the table noticed her as she stood weeping behind Jesus. She looked down at His dust-covered feet and then about the room for the basin and towel, but they had long since been removed. Then she had an idea and dropped to her knees.

She let her tears fall onto His feet and washed them. Then she did the most unspeakable thing imaginable: she pulled her head covering loose and began to wipe His feet with her hair. What did it matter to her that all of the righteous men present would presume her impurity by the act? She already was—and she would always remain—sinful in their eyes. Social conventions forbade her from offering the kiss of greeting to Jesus, so as a servant might a master, she began to kiss His feet.

As conversation at the table stilled, she felt their eyes and the weight of their judgment fall on her. How dare this sinful woman thwart their reproach of the young Rabbi! She would pay for her insolence!

She grasped the alabaster jar and deftly tapped it against the floor. As the seal cracked, the smell of the perfume filled the room. She poured the entire contents of it onto Jesus' feet.

Simon gazed haughtily across the table at Jesus. If He were truly a prophet, He would know that the woman touching Him was a sinner.

But Jesus did not rebuke her. He did not send her away. He turned to Simon instead.

"Simon, I have something to say to you that you might not like very much."

"Say it, Teacher," Simon responded.

"There was a creditor to whom two different men were in debt. The first man owed him five hundred denarii;* the second owed him only fifty. Neither man could pay him back, so he forgave both debts. Which man do you think loved him more?"

"I guess the one who was forgiven more," Simon said.

"Good answer. That is correct," Jesus answered.

Then, Jesus gestured toward the woman. *"Look at this woman,"* He said softly. *"I entered your house, Simon, and you didn't even give Me any water for*

My feet! This woman has washed My feet with her tears and dried them with her hair. You gave every man here a kiss of greeting except Me, but she has not stopped covering My feet with kisses. You did not anoint My head with oil, but she has anointed My feet with expensive perfume. She loves Me much, because she knows she has been forgiven much. Don't you see, Simon? If I reject sinners, that means I will have to reject you too!"[1]

Then Jesus turned to speak gently to the woman at His feet.

"Your faith has saved you; go in peace" (Luke 7:50).

Prayer

Savior,

What words can express my gratitude to You for covering my shame? What precious gift do I have to bring? You are the gentle Savior of those who are broken and weary. May I always be willing to enter into reproach for the privilege of expressing my love for You, for You have forgiven me much and set me free, and I adore You.

Amen

1. The conversation between Jesus and Simon here is the author's translation based on the work of Kenneth Bailey, *Jesus Through Middle Eastern Eyes*, InterVarsity Press, Downers Grove, IL, pg 256.

ADULTERESS

Who is a God like you,
    who pardons sin and forgives the transgression
    of the remnant of his inheritance?
You do not stay angry forever
    but delight to show mercy.
You will again have compassion on us;
    you will tread our sins underfoot
    and hurl all our iniquities into the depths of the sea.

MICAH 7:18–19

THE LONG NIGHT IN her cell had given her time to think, time to regret, and time to fear the terror that awaited her with the morning light. What a fool she had been—a fool to believe he loved her, a fool to tell herself over and again the lie she needed to believe the most . . .

"Just one more time."

As hard as she tried, she just could not get out of her mind the image of him walking away into the night, a bag of temple silver jingling in his hand as they led her alone to her condemnation. He never even looked back.

How exactly does one commit adultery alone? she laughed ruefully to herself. The religious leaders, however, did not seem especially worried about logistics. She *was* just a woman, after all.

She knew all too well the horrors she would endure with the sun's rising. She would be publicly accused and humiliated. Then she would likely die a painful death as neighbors and strangers alike tossed curses and stones at her from the secure anonymity of a mob.

The room lightened slowly until, at last, the first rays of morning sun began to filter into the cell from a narrow window near the ceiling. Moments later, the guards pushed open the heavy wooden door, crossed the room to where she was sitting, and roughly pulled her to her feet.

The Pharisees were waiting in the courtyard, resplendent in their rich, flowing robes. They preceded her into the street and began to call out her crime to the good citizens of Jerusalem.

"Adulteress! Caught in the very act!"

Soon a large crowd began following them. They shouted and spit at her as the guards harshly shoved her onward. She began sobbing in terror and shame, which seemed to anger the crowd all the more. Then she stumbled and fell.

"Get her up," someone snarled in disgust. The guards pulled her from the dust and shoved her forward once again.

To her dismay, she realized the mob was driving her straight to the temple.

Soon, they entered the temple gate, crossed the beautiful, patterned floor of the Court of Women, and went straight to where a crowd had already gathered around a seated Rabbi for an early morning lesson. They made her stand in the midst of the crowd before Him.

Shaking convulsively for a moment, she then collapsed to the ground with her face pressed to the dust before she was once again forced to her feet to stand, humiliated, before the crowd.

The Roman soldiers lining the roof of the cloister nearby tightened their grip on their swords and watched warily, ready to strike in a moment's notice if the scene boiled over into an uprising.

Tension filled the air as the leader of the Pharisees began walking around her, raising his hand to silence the mob. Soon her quiet whimpering was the only sound in the temple courts. The Pharisee turned to address the Rabbi, Jesus, in a voice loud enough for all to hear.

"Teacher, this woman was caught in adultery, in the very act. Now Moses, in the Law, commanded us that such should be stoned."

He paused and with just a hint of a smile asked, "But what do You say?" (John 8:4–5 NKJV).

She kept her eyes to the ground but could feel the heavy weight of the crowd's stares.

There was one Man, however, who refused to stare. Jesus did not answer the Pharisee, but remained in His seat and bent over to write in the dust.

The Pharisees and Sadducees would not be silenced so easily. They began interrogating Jesus, demanding that He answer their question. Would Jesus violate Roman law and send her to her death, or would He stand for moral injustice and let her go? It was a no-win situation, which is just what these leaders of the synagogue had been working to achieve. Besides, everyone knew Jesus had a terrible soft spot for sinners. For the Pharisees and Sadducees, victory was so close they could almost taste it.

Finally, Jesus lifted His finger from the dust and straightened up to face them and pronounce His verdict.

"Let any one of you who is without sin be the first to throw a stone at her" (John 8:7).

Then He bent over and began writing in the dirt again, signaling to them that the matter was settled.

A murmur passed through the crowd as the Pharisees whispered among themselves, trying to decide their next move.

Jesus wrote in the dust. The woman wept.

At the back of the group of leaders, the oldest Pharisee was the first to recognize that they were beaten and quietly slipped away.

> *Then, one by one, the others followed until only she was left standing before Jesus, awaiting His judgment.*

She was stunned. Moments before, a crowd had screamed for her blood, and somehow this Rabbi who did not even know her name had stepped into the Pharisees' crosshairs for her, to take her place as the target of their condemnation and rage. She knew the incident was not over for Him. They would not forget such a humiliating loss on their home turf.

Jesus straightened once again, looked at her, and softly asked, *"Woman, where are they? Has no one condemned you?"*

"No one, sir," she whispered through her tears.

"Then neither do I condemn you," He said. *"Go now and leave your life of sin"* (John 8:10–11).

Prayer

Light of the World,

Grant me the grace to withstand the wooing of the deceiver. Remind me daily that he preys on me when I am the most vulnerable, luring me into sin only to condemn me when I fall. By Your power may I quickly turn to You when my heart is broken, and may I find in You my deepest longings fulfilled. For in You I find blessing without sorrow; in You I find fullness of joy. Ever shine Your light into the darkness of my grief, my sin, my cavernous need . . .

Keep me near.

Amen

Healing at the Pool of Bethesda

"I will rescue the lame;
  I will gather the exiles.
I will give them praise and honor
  in every land where they have suffered shame.
At that time I will gather you;
  at that time I will bring you home.
I will give you honor and praise
  among all the peoples of the earth
when I restore your fortunes
    before your very eyes,"
    says the LORD.

ZEPHANIAH 3:19–20

TORCHLIGHT FLICKERED OFF THE sides of the moss-lined stone walls of the shaft. The workman looked up at the round patch of sky far above him and then switched the torch to his other hand before drying his palm on the front of his tunic. He reached up with his free hand, found in the wall the highest recess he could grasp, and hoisted himself upward, feeling with his foot for another hold that had been carved into the shaft. In this way he climbed step by step until he arrived at the pulley system. Once there, he secured the torch in its recess in the wall and paused to look at the two sluice gates* far below. He took a deep breath and grasped the ropes.

Up above, Jesus was just entering the columned, covered porticoes of the Pool of Bethesda.* Before Him stretched two pools divided by a central wall. The porches surrounding the pools were covered with the lame, sick, and diseased, each believing that healing powers lay in wait for the one who was first in the pool when the waters churned and turned red as blood. In the nearby Roman pools of Asclepius*—their god of healing— snakes that were believed to have curative powers were allowed to swim with the sick. The children of God had absorbed this pagan theology and mixed it in their *mikveh*.* No longer did they place all their hope for healing in God, but in the waters of Bethesda that bubbled and churned.

Jesus paused to look at the pitiful, suffering, and misguided masses before Him. Beyond the pools, just to the south, the temple rose toward the sky, its golden and white hues shining gloriously in the sunlight. Within these resplendent halls, the Teachers of the Law* sat in flowing robes debating the fine points of sanctity, oblivious to the teeming masses of suffering bodies so near the temple gates. These Teachers of the Law were proud to hold high the standard of holiness. Their pontification on the subject rang long and loud within the temple courts. Too loud, in fact, for them to be able to hear the cries of those suffering souls who surrounded and gazed into Bethesda's Pool, waiting in false hope.

But even if the teachers had heard, they would not have sullied their robes to lift a finger and help.

Jesus began walking among the suffering whose pallets were considered too unclean for the temple courts. Their moans and cries followed Him as they stretched their hands out high, begging for alms. His eyes roved from face to face, searching for the most desperate of them all.

For thirty-eight years this one particular man had waited. He had hoped, despaired, and hoped again as he'd watched the waters churn. He had suffered countless moments of crushing disappointment when someone else made it into the pool ahead of him.

The eyes of the Savior rested on this man.

The workman in the shaft beneath the central wall strained against the ropes, forcing them around the pulley. Far beneath him, the heavy sluice gates groaned and then slowly began to rise, releasing a rush of water from the reservoir of the northern pool and into the southern one. As the force of the water pushed against the walls of the shaft, it broke loose dark red soil from a fissure running through the rock, turning the water blood red. As the workman secured the rope to hold the sluice gate open, he heard a multitude of cries erupt from the pool above and a great splashing as desperate men threw themselves into the pool.

Jesus watched the man's eyes light up at the water's stirring . . . and then dim as he sank back on his pallet, turned his face to the wall, and pulled a blanket over his head.

Jesus knelt down beside him and placed a hand on his shoulder.

"Do you want to get well?" (John 5:6).

The man raised himself up onto his elbows, glanced up at Jesus, and then looked down at his mat and pile of beggar's coins. It was the only life he had ever known. He had no skill, no trade. How could he provide for himself apart from begging? He paused for a moment, looked at the once-again still waters of Bethesda, and turned his eyes to Jesus.

"Sir," he said, his voice breaking with frustration and long deferred hope, "I have no one to help me into the pool when the water is stirred. While I am trying to get in, someone else goes down ahead of me."

Jesus looked into his eyes and sighed deeply as His grip tightened on the man's shoulder, *"Get up! Pick up your mat and walk"* (John 5:7–8).

His legs, long withered and lifeless, grew strong as feeling returned to them. The man gasped, and his eyes filled with tears. He leaped to his feet, grasped his mat, and turned to say thanks, but his Healer was gone.

The man looked down at his good legs, wiggled his toes, and laughed softly to himself. Then he rolled up his mat and left the Pool of Bethesda behind. He stepped into the street, took a deep breath, and turned his face to the sky for a long moment before looking around from his new vantage point. The nearby temple caught his eye. He had never been able to go all the way inside Herod's magnificent temple with the other men because his mat was considered unclean, but today he would go. He would go and thank God for the amazing gift of a new beginning. He began to walk in the direction of the temple when he met a group of Jewish leaders on the way.

"Stop right there, man. What do you think you are doing?"

"I'm sorry?" he asked, perplexed.

"Why are you carrying that mat? Do you not know today is a Sabbath?"

"Oh, I'm carrying the mat because the Man who healed me told me to pick up my mat and walk."

It was a moment of wonder. Surely these teachers of Israel would want to know who had the power to heal the lame. Such an act bore the very fingerprints of God! But their minds were still entrenched in legalities, so they totally missed the wonder of the Almighty. After all, their legalism was never about the glory of God but forever about the glory of man as he strove to take God's place.

"And who is this who told you to pick up your mat and walk?"

"I'm not sure," he responded. "He's gone."

Due to threat of stoning, the bewildered man abandoned his mat and continued on to the temple courts.

He stopped to bathe in the *mikveh* before walking for the very first time up the lofty steps and into the expansive Court of the Gentiles.* Moments later, he stood before the beautiful bronze Gates of Nicanor.* He closed his eyes and began to whisper his heartfelt thanks to God.

A strong, calm voice beside him broke into his reverie.

"See, you are well again."

The man turned to look into the face of his Healer, Jesus.

The external healing had taken place at the pool,
but an inner healing was still needed.

"Stop sinning or something worse may happen to you" (John 5:14).

Worse? Worse than thirty-eight years paralyzed and hopeless in Bethesda's porticoes? When he had lain beside the pool, Jesus had asked if he wanted to be well. Now Jesus was offering the man an inner restoration. The man nodded solemnly. He was ready to live his life for the glory of God. He had met Jesus and would never be the same.

Prayer ———————————————————

My Healer,

    Is it possible that I have grown to cherish my wounds because they are familiar to me? Could it be that I value the illusion of control over the surrender that would render me whole? Convict me when I choose the familiarity of brokenness over Your healing touch. Give me the courage to abandon myself fully to Your healing power and to the great and blessed unknown that awaits me on the other side of my restoration.

                                Amen

LIKE SCARLET . . . AS WHITE AS SNOW

"Come now, let us settle the matter,"
says the LORD.
"Though your sins are like scarlet,
they shall be as white as snow;
though they are red as crimson,
they shall be like wool."

ISAIAH 1:18

"OK, EVERYONE, LET'S SWITCH sides. My arm is getting tired," Nathaniel said. He leaned over my stretcher and looked me in the eyes when he spoke to me. "Hold on, Judah. We will be back on our way in a moment." He gave me a brief, reassuring smile before turning to the other three. Slowly, they lowered me to the ground before trading positions around the corners of my mat.

Thomas dusted off his hands before bending down to grasp his end of the pole and frowned. "Are you sure about the house, Nathaniel?"

"Everyone is saying the Healer is staying with Peter the fisherman. His house is over near the synagogue. I have a feeling there will be a crowd. It should be pretty difficult to miss."

Jacob looked up at Nathaniel and then took a firm grip on his end of the pole. "You're right about the crowd. We had better get moving."

Andrew grinned mischievously at me and playfully swatted my lifeless calf before grabbing his end of the stretcher again. "I hope you slept well last night, my friend," he said, "because we are going to have you dancing on those legs all night tonight. We are long overdue a celebration." I smiled back at him, both amused and touched by his outrageous optimism.

Andrew, of course, had no way of knowing how elusive sleep had become for me. It was one of the great surprises of paralysis. It turns out that since the body lies sedentary every day, it forgets to sleep when appropriate. Night after night I lay awake in the darkness listening to the sounds of sleeping Capernaum—the Sea of Galilee lapping against the shore, the fishing boats creaking in their moorings. On good nights, the full moon lit up the inside of our home just enough for me to pass the time by visually tracing the branches that crisscrossed the thatched ceiling above my head.

Most nights, however, I stared wide-eyed into the darkness, hour after hour counting my father's rhythmic snores in the next room as I waited for morning.

And every night, as the darkness draped heavily around me, I wrestled with the ghosts of regret and shame. I lay in a physical prison with nothing to do but think. I once heard a rabbi say that illness is God's judgment on sin, and on those nights no one could have convinced me otherwise. After all, what better punishment for sin than to turn a young man's body to stone yet leave his mind intact to contemplate all the mistakes he has made?

I learned to weep silently in the dark, through the watches of the night, as I poured out my repentance to God. I begged Him for mercy, for just one more chance to live my life normally. Hour after hour, I mourned before God until I wearied myself from grief, and sleep claimed me at last.

Nathaniel grasped his end of the stretcher. "Ok, friends, let's lift on the count of three. One, two, three . . ." I gasped involuntarily as the stretcher swayed and lifted into the air.

"Don't worry, Judah," Andrew teased me. "We haven't come this far to drop you in the street."

I grinned at him and then turned my head from side to side to glance up at my friends, but I could see little except the muscular forearms of the two closest to my head. I craned my neck up and looked down at my own body, once as strong as theirs. Now my arms and legs were birdlike. Muscles had melted away to leave skin clinging to bone. Angry red pressure sores peeked out from the sides of my knees. I was told there were even larger sores at the base of my back and on my shoulder blades. They most certainly would have been excruciatingly painful—if I could feel them. My mother worried about them incessantly, washing and soothing them with poultices. She enlisted help from whoever was near when she needed to roll me into a new position, her attempt to keep new sores from forming. I was helpless, and I felt like a burden to everyone.

I was well aware that not all my friends were willing or able to remain faithful to someone in my condition; many, in fact, weren't. Some of my friends seemed afraid of me after the accident, as if my misfortune might somehow rub off on them. Besides, it was so much easier to forget about me than to wait with me for my ultimate death. And this injury *would* eventually kill me. It was just taking its time.

But these four friends were different. We had been babies together, then toddlers. As boys, we were together when our fathers taught us to fish, and we sat together at the feet of the same rabbi as we memorized the Law. We grew into young men together, and all of us were planning our betrothals and looking forward to establishing our own homes. We always assumed we would raise our sons side by side the way our parents had. Then, for me, it was all over in a moment.

They could have turned away from me, but they didn't. They came and sat beside my bed, helped me remember better times, and insisted I dream of a future when I would be whole again. When I crumbled under the weight of my lost dignity and wanted to die, they refused to allow me to wallow in self-pity.

> *Now they were giving me the greatest gift of all: they were believing for me when I had no faith left.*

I closed my eyes and tried to breathe deeply as the stretcher jostled along the streets of Capernaum toward their hope for me, a hope I was far too afraid to entertain. A moment later, we turned the corner and came to an abrupt stop.

"Is that the crowd for the Healer?" Jacob asked, astonished. "We can't even get to the door of the courtyard."

A worried silence fell over them. Finally, Nathaniel spoke. "Let's take Judah over to the steps of the synagogue. You three can rest there with him for a moment while I walk around the house to see if there is any other way in. Perhaps there is a secondary courtyard in the back."

Soon I was resting at the foot of the basalt* steps of the synagogue as my friends flanked me protectively. Andrew placed his hand on the top of my head for a moment, and then we settled down to await Nathaniel's return.

When Nathaniel reached the house across the street, he saw the people pressed against the wall surrounding the home in an effort to catch a glimpse of the Miracle Worker. Occasionally, an excited cry erupted as a healing took place from within the crowded house.

Nathaniel returned and knelt down beside me to address us.

"There is a second courtyard, but it too is filled. I have an idea, though. There is a large central room with several other rooms adjoining both that larger room and the courtyards. I'm pretty sure the Healer is in the large room. It looks like the crowds are funneling into that area. The large room also has two small rooms immediately adjoining it, and although there are a lot of people in the courtyards, no one is next to those two small rooms. I think we should go there and climb onto the roof. Once we are up there, we can go over to the main room and pull apart the branches and mud-mortar of the roof. When we have a hole big enough, we will lower Judah, on his mat, by ropes directly in front of the Healer."

Andrew smiled, his eyes twinkling with mischief. "I love it!" he said. "Let's do it."

Moments later, they carried my stretcher to the ground next to the house. Both Andrew and Jacob grasped one end of my mat and lifted me off the stretcher before placing me on the ground as Nathaniel and Thomas unwound the ropes from the poles. With confident fishermen's hands they wound the ropes around my mat, tying knots and forming a sling with long ends of rope. When they finished, everyone stepped back for a moment to survey their work.

Thomas spoke next. "Nathaniel, you and I probably have the most upper body strength. I think we should go onto the roof."

"Agreed," Nathaniel said.

Both men grasped the edge of the roofline just above their heads as Andrew and Jacob laced their hands to give them a foothold for a boost. In one swift movement, they were on the roof. Immediately, they lay on their stomachs and reached down for the ends of the rope. Andrew leaned over and picked me up in his arms like a child, sling and all, as Jacob grabbed the ends of the rope to hand me up to Nathaniel and Thomas. My heart pounded in my chest, and I tried to take deep breaths to calm myself as the ropes grew taut and Andrew released his grip from beneath me. Once again he leaned over and looked long into my eyes. This time all laughter was gone.

"We aren't going to let you fall, Judah.
I promise you. Can you trust me?"

I nodded and closed my eyes as my friends, straining, began to pull the ropes, and I began ascending to the roof.

Once we were all on the roof, Nathaniel motioned for the others to crouch low, out of sight of the crowd below, and wait quietly. Silently, he crept toward the main room. Once there, he placed his ear to the branches and dried mud to listen. He paused and then moved a few feet to the right, listened again, and then motioned for the other men to bring me to where he was. Jacob stayed with me, steadying me while the other men began to pry the branches loose with their bare hands. They were fishermen, and their hands were calloused from their labors. But the branches were rough, and soon deep red gashes traced the dust and grime on their fingers. The work was not easy, but they were determined. In a moment, as the hole grew larger, we could hear cries from the astonished crowd inside.

Nathaniel looked into the room below and motioned for Andrew and Thomas to stop digging. Then he crawled the short distance to where I was and looked into my face.

"Are you ready, my friend?"

"Yes, friend. I am ready."

He and Jacob moved me to the opening where the other two men were already positioned on their stomachs to lower me into the room. I closed my eyes as I saw their hands grab the ropes. Slowly, I began the descent.

Then I felt myself stop. I opened my eyes and looked up. Directly above me was the face of Jesus. He turned from me to look at my friends, gazing down through the roof above Him, and smiled, shaking His head in wonder. Then Jesus turned back to me and looked into my eyes for a long moment. He seemed to look far past my broken body and into the depths of my tortured soul. His eyes were filled with compassion. He placed His hand on my head and, with great gentleness, spoke to my deepest need.

"Son, your sins are forgiven" (Mark 2:5).

Forgiven. I took a long shuddering breath as tears rolled down my cheeks. *Forgiven . . .*

Somewhere behind me in the crowd there arose a murmur of disapproval. Jesus frowned, turned quickly to look toward the sound, and spoke to those seated there.

"Why are you thinking these things? Which is easier: to say to this paralyzed man, 'Your sins are forgiven,' or to say, 'Get up, take your mat and walk'? But I want you to know that the Son of Man has authority on earth to forgive sins" (Mark 2:8–10).

Then He turned back to me.

"I tell you, get up, take your mat and go home" (Mark 2:11).

How can I describe what happened next? Power coursed through my body. Immediately, I felt my arms again, my legs, my feet. I looked down to see withered limbs grow strong and muscular, and right before my eyes sores faded away. I looked at Jesus and laughed in wonder. Then I sat up and looked down at my hands as I clenched and unclenched my fists. Next, I rolled my ankles, wiggled my toes.

I lifted trembling hands to my face and began to weep, and then laugh, and then weep again.

*In one horrible moment an accident had taken
everything away. In the blink of an eye and by
His word alone, Jesus had restored it all.*

Jesus laughed and looked up at my friends as they gazed, awestruck, from their perch above. I stood to my feet, and their reverie was broken. They began to scream and cheer, hugging one another as they scrambled for the edge of the roof and the ground. I knelt to the floor beside Jesus and poured out my gratitude and tears.

As the crowd around me broke into praise, my mat on the floor caught my attention. I picked it up, placed it on my shoulder, and stood to my feet. For so long, it had carried me, but now I would carry it home. I was a prisoner no more.

Prayer ——————————————————————

Great Healer,

No matter how great my physical need, my need for forgiveness and mercy runs deeper. So my heart cries out for redemption. In You, Precious Savior, I find peace for my sin-weary soul. May I forever be mindful of and grateful for Your grace.

And when my way grows long and my faith wears thin, grant me the gift of godly friends who will hold onto hope when I cannot, friends who will lead me onward.

Amen

ALL THINGS POSSIBLE

The Boy with a Deaf and Mute Demon

*Have mercy on me, L*ORD*, for I am faint;*
*   heal me, L*ORD*, for my bones are in agony.*
My soul is in deep anguish.
*   How long, L*ORD*, how long?*
*Turn, L*ORD*, and deliver me;*
*   save me because of your unfailing love.*

PSALM 6:2–4

"There you are," his father whispered as he held the boy's face in his hands. He stared deeply into his son's eyes, clear and shining for only an instant. Then, through tears . . .

"Oh, I've missed you, my son!"

The boy's eyes held his, and his face lit with a smile. The boy wrapped his arms around his father's waist and lay his head on his shoulder.

"*Abba* . . ."

It was heaven. For a moment. Then the darkness crept back, seeping in around the edges of the boy's beautiful dark eyes until they were once again overtaken by a flat and blank stare. His face went slack, then a scream followed by a hellish outburst that was all too familiar.

Those joyous moments were so rare and beautiful, the father desperately clung to them—they gave him the will to take another step, to keep hoping, to just hold on. Sometimes, when the day seemed especially dark, he would call up a memory of one of those sweet days when his son's demon granted him a brief reprieve. Doing so helped the father stay sane.

Shaking his head to clear it, the father returned his attention to the crowd surrounding them. Rabbi Jesus' disciples, red faced, anxious, and frustrated, were on one side. Across from them the local teachers of the Law were loudly pontificating. All around them, a crowd had gathered to watch the show. This father and his boy were stage center, silent players in a tragedy.

The boy's eyes were blank beneath his furrowed brow. Dark curls swept the collar of his robe and framed a beautiful face where, day by day, the more angular lines of a young man were replacing the soft contours of boyhood. A large burn scar—shiny, folded layers of pink and tan—covered his right temple and stretched from his ear to his eye. It was only one of many scars on his body. Scars covered his arms, legs, feet, and hands. A large red scar dripped across his upper back like a crimson ink spill.

The father glanced down at his son's hand in his. The boy stood, completely unresponsive except for the white-knuckled grip he kept on his daddy's hand. Perhaps it was a sign that somewhere deep down the boy understood who his father was, maybe even drew comfort from his presence. The father noticed how large his son's hand had become. He had grown bigger and stronger by the day, so each time the spirit threw his son into the fire or the water, his father found it more and more difficult to restrain him.

'The father also noticed the scars on his own hands, testimony to the countless times he had reached into flames of fire to save his son.

There they stood, one burn-scarred hand clinging tightly to another. The crowd roared around them, debating theology and the hopelessness of the situation, but the son remained unresponsive, as though he heard nothing. Reaching out to gently caress the scarred hand he held in his own, the father fought back tears. It had not always been this way. At one time he had held great hope for his firstborn son—before the darkness descended on the happy, affectionate toddler; before the father realized this tormented, sick boy would be his only child.

The voice of one of the teachers of the Law broke through the father's reverie. "Of course, you could not cast the spirit out of the boy! It is preposterous to even try. To cast out an evil spirit, it is necessary to first obtain the *name* of the spirit. This is a deaf and mute spirit. It is, therefore, quite impossible to ask it for its name. Consequently, to cast out this spirit is an act only Messiah Himself could accomplish. The boy's situation is quite hopeless."

Hopeless.

No other word had been more often associated with his boy, and the father was ashamed to admit that much of the time he himself had been the one to give life to the word. The word stalked his footsteps, haunted his dreams, and silenced his prayers. It looped in his head over and again until he thought he would lose his mind. There were even times in the dark of night that he and his wife had said the word aloud through exhausted tears.

Hopeless. They shouldn't have come.

Then a voice broke into his despair.

"What are you arguing with them about?" Someone asked (Mark 9:16).

Jesus had arrived to find the chaos of the crowd. The father gazed at Him for a moment as relief flooded the disciples' faces and the teachers of the Law prepared themselves afresh for battle. But neither group was afforded a chance to speak. The desperate father in their midst was all too anxious to reach the Rabbi who healed.

The father released his son's hand, then pushed through the crowd to fall on his knees before Jesus.

"Rabbi, I beg You, please take a look at my son. He is my only child. He is possessed by a spirit that inflicts him with seizures. He screams, falls on the ground, foams at the mouth, and becomes rigid. The spirit also throws him into the fire and water to try to kill him. It almost never leaves him and is completely destroying him before our eyes. I begged Your disciples to help him, but they couldn't do it."[1]

"You unbelieving generation," Jesus replied, *"how long shall I stay with you? How long shall I put up with you? Bring the boy to me"* (Mark 9:19).

But just as the father began leading his son to Jesus, he felt the boy's grip slacken and fall away. His heart sank.

"No . . ."

He turned to look at his son. A slow, gleeful smile crossed the boy's face before he tilted his head back and screamed. The boy fell to the ground and the father fell with him, trying to protect his son's head as it thrashed back and forth. The father reached out with the edge of his robe to wipe away first the foam from the boy's mouth and then the blood that came as his son bit his tongue in the midst of the seizure. The father held his face close to his son's and whispered words of comfort, all to no avail.

Jesus knelt down beside them and placed a hand on the man's shoulder. *"How long has he been like this?"* (Mark 9:21).

Tears streamed down the father's face. "He's been like this since he was a little child. Please, please, if You can do *anything* for us, please help us."

Jesus' grip on the father's shoulder tightened, and he looked from the depths of frantic despair into the eyes of sure hope.

"'If you can'?" said Jesus. *"Everything is possible for one who believes"* (Mark 9:23).

Oh, how he wanted to believe. He was just so weary, so worn down by grief. He had so little strength left.

The father's body shook with sobs as he cried out, "I do believe; help me overcome my unbelief!" (Mark 9:24).

Jesus looked up to see a large crowd running to the scene and then, turning back to the boy, did what the teachers of the Law insisted only Messiah could do. *"You deaf and mute spirit,"* he said, *"I command you, come out of him and never enter him again"* (Mark 9:25).

The boy screamed and convulsed again. Then the spirit was gone, and the boy was utterly still.

"He's dead," someone in the crowd proclaimed.

But Jesus reached out, took the boy's hand, and helped him to his feet. The boy turned to his father with clear and shining eyes. When a smile broke through his father's tears, the boy returned it. The father took his child's face in his hands.

"Oh, how I've missed you, my son!"

It was a moment rare and beautiful. The boy would never be lost again. Hope had come to stay.

Prayer ——————————————————————————

Messiah,

Nothing is too hard for You. Please give me the faith to trust You even when everything I see and hear declares that all hope is lost. Enter into the midnight of my despair, compassionate Christ.

I believe. Help my unbelief.

Amen

1. The author's translation, drawing from all scriptural accounts.

THE CENTURION'S SERVANT

---

*Nevertheless, there will be no more gloom for those
who were in distress. In the past he humbled the
land of Zebulun and the land of Naphtali, but in
the future he will honor Galilee of the nations,
by the Way of the Sea, beyond the Jordan—*

> *The people walking in darkness*
> *have seen a great light;*
> *on those living in the land of deep darkness*
> *a light has dawned.*

ISAIAH 9:1–2

FOUR JEWISH ELDERS STOOD in vigilance on a street corner in Capernaum's center. Each man wore around his shoulders a white prayer shawl trimmed in blue and fringed with tassels. Long gray beards brushed the front of their robes as the men, looking back and forth, surveyed the city before them. To their right rose an eight-foot-high seawall that supported the twenty-five-hundred-foot-long promenade. The promenade was bustling with fishermen, merchants, and townspeople as they made their way to and from the waterfront going about their business. A series of piers, some straight and some curved, stretched out from the promenade into the Sea of Galilee and provided fishing boats with precious shelter from the frequent violent storms that arose on the lake. Several boats were there now, bobbing to and fro in their moorings, as men laughed and joked while unloading the previous night's catch.

The streets were busy as the citizens of Capernaum went about their daily business alongside merchants from all over the world. These merchants were drawn into Capernaum's gates due to her proximity to the International Highway.* Local merchants whose baskets were filled with olives, dried fish, and grain mingled with tradesmen carrying more exotic wares. Their spices and silks were from lands as unfamiliar as their dialects that mingled and drifted on the steady breeze from the lake.

The elders turned toward the sound of two foreign merchants arguing over their wares. They watched the men as their faces reddened and voices rose. For a moment it appeared they might come to blows, but then two Roman soldiers rounded the corner on their way to the shore. Peace was restored immediately, simply by the appearance of the two men. Capernaum was an observant Jewish city, faithful to God's law, but one with a strong Roman presence; a garrison of Roman soldiers had been stationed there to protect this valuable city of imports. The two soldiers continued on toward the shore and the merchants dispersed, leaving the elders alone on the street corner.

All of the buildings in Capernaum were of the same rough, black basalt and thatch-roof construction. Most homes were modest, built as a series of small rooms around two central courtyards. One building in the center of town eclipsed all these others. Made from the same basalt stone, this building was ornately carved and supported by walls four feet thick. Inside, cobbled basalt floors stretched beneath the breathtaking gray granite columns that lined the interior of the structure. As the Jewish elders turned to gaze in the direction of their beloved synagogue, one reached up under the sleeve of his robe to gently stroke the leather phylactery tied around his arm.

Just then they spotted the young Rabbi and His men walking toward the synagogue, and with as much haste as decorum would permit men of their age and station, they made pursuit. A moment later, they stood before Jesus in the shadow of the synagogue and began to make their arguments.

"Please, Rabbi, we have a request. We come on behalf of the Roman centurion who is in charge of this city. He asked us to speak to You for him. His servant is paralyzed and suffering terribly. It is the centurion's respectful request that You come heal the man."

Jesus and the disciples gazed silently at the men for a moment as they considered the strange request. Rome was Israel's hated oppressor, so most law-abiding Jews would have nothing to do with assisting a Roman, especially a Roman centurion. Not willingly at least. How even more remarkable that a group of Jewish elders would approach Rabbi Jesus on behalf of this man!

Rome, of course, was not Capernaum's first oppressor. The city had a long history of invasion and brutality. Capernaum's location, so near the International Highway, was both a blessing and a curse. The same proximity that brought trade into her gates allowed invaders into her streets as well.

The Assyrians breeched her walls first, and under Hasmonaean* rule the Jewish population living there was almost annihilated. Later, during the revolt against Rome in 38 BC, Herod the Great slaughtered entire families of Jewish rebels in the nearby Caves of Arbela.* He lowered his men, armed with long hooks, over the edges of the cliffs to reach the lofty caves on the mountainside. The soldiers then used their weapons to snare the men, women, and children inside the caves and toss them over the precipice to their deaths.

Truly, when Jesus, the Messiah, chose Capernaum as His adopted hometown, a great light was shining in the darkness.[1]

―――――――

As they waited for Jesus to answer, the Jewish elders looked at Him and then back up at the beautiful building behind them.

"This man deserves to have you do this, because he loves our nation and has built our synagogue!" they pleaded (Luke 7:4–5).

Jesus had been walking along Capernaum's streets that morning, returning home after teaching, but now His plans had changed. Of course He would go! As He turned to follow the Jewish leaders out the city gate toward the centurion's home, a crowd gathered in His wake in anticipation of another miraculous healing.

―――――――

The centurion's face was grim as he stood over the bed where his servant lay. Looking up at the centurion, the poor man's eyes were wide with terror and locked on his master's in a silent plea for help. His breath was rapid and shallow with suffering. The centurion placed a comforting hand on his forehead. Then, cradling the back of the servant's neck with one hand, he lifted the sick man's head and raised a cup of water to his mouth. Slowly, he dribbled a few drops past the dry, cracked lips and onto his parched tongue before gently returning his head to his mat.

Tears began running down the servant's face, and he closed his eyes.

The centurion turned and nodded to another servant standing nearby. "Give him a few drops of water every few minutes, but not too much or he will choke."

"Yes, master."

He bent down and placed his hand on the servant's head once more and then walked from the room.

A soldier awaited him in the hall.

"Yes?"

"Rabbi Jesus is on His way, sir."

Rabbi Jesus was coming to his house?

The centurion acknowledged the soldier with a nod, then walked into his reception room and over to the window where he stared down the road leading to Capernaum. He reached down and absentmindedly ran his hand along the crest of his helmet that was resting on a stone table at his side. What was he going to do?

He desperately wanted his suffering, paralyzed servant to be healed, and he believed Rabbi Jesus was his best chance.

But he also knew enough about Jewish culture to understand that it wasn't acceptable for Jesus—or any Jewish teacher—to enter a Gentile's home.

The Jews had strict guidelines regarding separation from Gentiles: Jews believed that entering a Gentile home caused them to become defiled.

In fact, the Jews believed that on the day Messiah came there would be a great feast, but a feast that would exclude all Gentiles. The centurion knew that, no matter how much he grew to love Israel, no matter how beautiful a synagogue he built in Capernaum, and no matter how grateful the Jews might be, they still considered him and his home unclean. He simply couldn't expect any rabbi to defile himself by coming inside his house.

Frowning as he considered the predicament, the centurion looked down at the short, vinewood staff in his hand. The staff was no weapon, but it was an indisputable symbol of his rank, his authority. As he ran his thumb along the top, he turned to stare back down the road to Capernaum again. Then he called for a soldier.

"I need you to take a message to Rabbi Jesus."

Jesus and the crowd paused in the road at the sight of three armed Roman guards in the distance. Moments later, the guards stood before them— "We have a message from our master for Rabbi Jesus. This is what he says:

> "Lord, don't trouble yourself, for I do not deserve to have you come under my roof. That is why I did not even consider myself worthy to come to you. But say the word, and my servant will be healed. For I myself am a man under authority, with soldiers under me. I tell this one, 'Go,' and he goes; and that one, 'Come,' and he comes. I say to my servant, 'Do this,' and he does it." (Luke 7:6–8)

Jesus shook His head in amazement and smiled. He turned to the crowd behind Him, to people entrenched in their idea of who was and who wasn't worthy of the kingdom of God, and began to speak to them.

"Truly I tell you, I have not found anyone in Israel with such great faith. I say to you that many will come from the east and the west, and will take their places

at the feast with Abraham, Isaac and Jacob in the kingdom of heaven. But the subjects of the kingdom will be thrown outside, into the darkness, where there will be weeping and gnashing of teeth" (Matthew 8:10–12).

The Jewish crowd gasped when they heard this scandalous proclamation. Was Rabbi Jesus really stating that acceptance into God's kingdom had nothing to do with paternity or nationality? Would they, the children of Israel, be judged by a different standard completely? Could the kingdom of God be a different kind of kingdom than they had long believed in and expected?

As the centurion stood at the window watching for the return of his men, he heard a commotion from the other room—shouting, laughter, and cries of joy. He closed his eyes, smiled, and whispered his thanksgiving. Then he turned to greet his servant who had indeed been made whole again by the power of Rabbi Jesus' word.

Prayer

Messiah,

I am so glad that the keys to Your kingdom are not gained through paternity, nationality, skin color, or denominational creed. Thank You that the citizens of Your kingdom are admitted on the basis of our simple faith as we cast our hope on Your great redemption. What a joyous day it will be when, at last, all swords are beaten into plowshares[2] and all the nations gather at Your table, praising the name of Jesus to the glory of God the Father. Come quickly, Lord Jesus. May it even be today.

Amen

1. Isaiah 9:2
2. Isaiah 2:4

THE MASTER VINTNER

———

*On this mountain the L*ORD *Almighty will prepare*
　　　a feast of rich food for all peoples,
a banquet of aged wine—
　　　the best of meats and finest of wines.
On this mountain he will destroy
　　　the shroud that enfolds all peoples,
the sheet that covers all nations;
　　　he will swallow up death forever.
*The Sovereign L*ORD *will wipe away the tears*
　　　from all faces;
he will remove his people's disgrace
　　　from all the earth.
*The L*ORD *has spoken.*

ISAIAH 25:6–8

THE LAMPS HAD BEEN lit. Platters of olives, roasted lamb, stuffed grape leaves, and dates stood at the ready next to row after row of amphorae* filled with wine. The guests chatted among themselves in quiet but joyful tones when, at last, someone hushed them.

"They are coming!"

Moments later the groom entered the gate wearing a white linen robe trimmed in blue. A ceremonial crown rested on his head. His new bride, still veiled, accompanied him. She too was enrobed in her finest. Gold bangles jingled upon her wrists. She was beautifully adorned for her groom.

The groom extended his hand to his bride and led her into the house. As a reverent hush fell over their family and friends, he spread a corner of his cloak over her shoulders symbolizing his commitment to protect and care for her before proclaiming for all to hear: "This is my wife, and I am her husband for all eternity."

He took her by the hand, and the lovers were excused to be alone as their wedding celebration began.

Eventually, of course, the happy couple rejoined the party as its rightful king and queen, but there was no rush. The event would last a full seven days. Jesus, His family, and some of His disciples were among those happily taking part in the feast.

And that feast was a tremendous social responsibility: the couple's families were expected to provide generously for a proper celebration. For days, all went well. Delicious food was plentiful and wine flowed, but then the unthinkable happened.

Two of the servants bustled into a side room where wine amphorae lined the wall. They walked to the nearest one, grasped the handles, and prepared to strain against the weight only to find it far too light. It was empty. Frowning, the men turned to the next amphora and found only dregs in the bottom. As they walked down the line of containers, they rapped each of them with their knuckles. Again and again, a hollow echo rang throughout the room.

Their eyes wide with alarm, they rushed out of the room to deliver the news—they were out of wine!

The disaster had to be brought to the attention of the groom's mother immediately, and when it was, the woman's joy instantly changed to horror. Tears filled her eyes, and she began to wring her hands.

Seeing her distress, Mary asked quietly as to the nature of the dilemma. She listened, patted the woman's arm, and asked her to wait. She knew Someone who might be able to help.

As she turned to leave, she motioned to the servants to follow her. She scanned the faces of those reclined along the triclinium table in the main room. He was not there. Then she made her way into the courtyard and found Him enjoying the party with His friends. She approached her son, cleared her throat, and leaned in close to His ear.

"They have no more wine," she said.

Jesus turned to look at her for a moment and then quietly replied, *"Woman, why do you involve me? My hour has not yet come."*

Mary simply turned to the servants.

"Do whatever he tells you" (John 2:3–5).

Jesus looked about the courtyard, and His eyes fell on six limestone water jars kept for ceremonial washing. Each could hold twenty to thirty gallons of water.

Costly limestone jars . . . The backbreaking labor required to fill them . . . All to be poured out in homage to the traditions of the fathers that had nothing to do with God's heart. Yet the Pharisees were so concerned about breaking one of God's laws that they had established fences or hedges around each law. The idea was to place enough of these traditions around each law so that the law itself would never be broken. But what began as a noble desire for holiness eventually took on a life of its own as neighbor began judging neighbor on how well each kept the traditions. Over time, the inevitable happened: the Pharisees fell into the trap of legalism. They would define the sin, judge at will, and lay the whole burden on their fellow man. This practice had reached the point that not even a wedding celebration was spared the crushing yoke of tradition.

Jesus turned to the servants and motioned to the jars. *"Fill the jars with water."*

The servants quickly began doing as they were told. When the last purification jar was filled to the brim, the servants returned for further instructions.

"Now," He told them, *"draw some out and take it to the master of the banquet"* (John 2:7–8).

One of the servants grasped a large pot by the handle and thrust it beneath the surface of the water in the purification jar. When he raised it again, the water that ran from the lip of the pot and down his hand was dark, and the sweet aroma of wine wafted through the air. The servant's eyes widened as he called for a serving pitcher and carefully filled it.

The master of the banquet was a corpulent man whose full beard cascaded in waves over his rich robes. He was engaged in a lively conversation with the diminutive older man next to him, but he would occasionally pick up his empty goblet and glance disapprovingly at the dregs in the bottom. As soon as the servant arrived at his side and filled the goblet, the man reached for it without looking at it, without interrupting his conversation, and took a sip.

The servants watched breathlessly from the back of the room as his eyes widened, and although the man next to him chattered on, it was the goblet that now had the banquet master's full attention. As he swirled the wine in the cup beneath the lamplight, he observed the depth of its color. He lifted it to his nose and breathed in the scent of vanilla and clove. He closed his eyes, took another sip, and savored hints of berries, cherries, and plums.

He set the goblet on the table, called the groom to his side, laughed, and gave him a joyous slap on the back.

"Everyone brings out the choice wine first and then the cheaper wine after the guests have had too much to drink; but you have saved the best till now" (John 2:10).

Prayer

Merciful Savior,

Forgive me for sacrificing joy and stealing it from others because I was too proud to receive Your gifts humbly. I have been guilty of building fences around my own idea of holiness—for myself and others—because I want control more than I want to trust. Please show me where I have set myself up as god, honoring tradition more than Your heart.

Most of all, forgive me for misrepresenting You as stingy and condemning when, in truth, You are the Giver of every good and perfect gift.[1] You, my Jesus, are the Master Vintner, and I joyfully worship You.

Amen

1. James 1:17

PLAYING THE TRUMPET

The Widow's Mite

"Do not mistreat or oppress a foreigner, for you were foreigners in Egypt.

"Do not take advantage of the widow or the fatherless. If you do and they cry out to me, I will certainly hear their cry."

EXODUS 22:21–23

She took the last step of the staircase ascending the Temple Mount and paused to gaze out across the expansive Court of the Gentiles, already crowded with pilgrims. The people moving steadily toward her moved according to tradition: enter from the right and exit to the left. Only those who were under Temple discipline would go against the flow of traffic.

Or those in mourning.

She self-consciously brushed the skirt of her coarse, black, goat-hair widow's garment with the trembling fingers of her left hand and clenched her right fist a bit tighter. There in her palm she felt the edges of two copper coins, thin and hard, press into her skin.

Two mites. It was almost nothing, but it was all she had.

She squinted into the already fierce Middle Eastern sun hanging in a cloudless blue sky, took a deep breath, and stepped into the crowded court of Herod the Great's magnificent temple. To the left, the temple rose breathtakingly above all else—a magnificent structure of white marble and gold, roofed with cedar. The Court of Women, also known as the Court of the Treasury, was straight ahead, but it seemed impossibly far away as she moved against the flow of humanity. Over and again the worshippers who crossed her path offered the same greeting as they recognized the vestiges of her bereavement: "May He who dwells in this house bring you comfort."

Comfort. If they only knew . . . She was learning many lessons in the wake of her husband's passing, and comfort was most certainly among them, but it was not the first. Before comfort came the far more difficult lesson of trust. At first, her days and nights had been a whirlwind of searing pain, rending loss, and blinding terror. But then her tears had stilled enough that she could listen, and her heart had quieted enough that she could remember. She was strengthened as she recalled God's past deliverances, the stories of the ancient Jewish fathers, and the countless words of the prophets and the psalms that had rung throughout the synagogues of her childhood. And so, a journey of trust began as she recited from memory:

> Do not put your trust in princes,
>> in human beings, who cannot save.
> When their spirit departs, they return to the ground;
>> on that very day their plans come to nothing.
>
> PSALM 146:3–4

It was easy for a woman in her day to put a vast amount of trust in the security of a husband, but life had taught her with brutal efficiency just how quickly all that security could be stripped away. All men, even *good* men, returned to the ground, and the day they do, the best of their plans vanish like the morning dew beneath the rising sun.

She glanced at the majestic columns of the Court of Women ahead and then, with her eyes, followed their graceful lines to the far end where the fifteen semicircular steps, one for each of the Psalms of Ascent,* rose to the Gates of Nicanor. On festival days the courts would be bright with lamp-light and filled with music and dance as the Levites lined the steps singing hymns of praise. Beyond the massive doors was the temple itself. The size of the stones alone were enough to invoke awe in anyone who saw them. Truly, Herod the Great built the temple with astonishing grandeur, but that was not the limit of his extraordinary architectural accomplishments. He also built Caesarea Maritima,* a city to rival the glories of Rome but a city without a natural harbor. So, out of pure determination, might, and ingenuity, Herod sculpted an artificial one on the floor of the sea. When he longed for the security of a fortress with all the comforts of home, he built

Masada* in the middle of the desert. Then, to ensure that all Jerusalem never forgot he was always watching her, Herod moved a mountain to build the conical fortress palace that was his namesake, Herodium.* Through mortar and stone he sought to be a god, and yet he too was a man. And when he died, he returned to the ground like all other men.

Pausing for a moment, the widow raised her left hand to shield her eyes from the sun. The Court of Women was only a few steps away. She could already see the thirteen shofarot,* or collection boxes, that lined the court. The light of the sun, now high in the sky, was reflecting off the metal shofar-shaped tubes affixed to the top of the boxes where the donations were deposited. Each time the worshippers dropped their donations down the shofar* and into the box below, a loud, distinctive noise rang throughout the temple courts. The larger the donation, the louder the shofar rang. As a result, this act of giving had come to be known as "playing the trumpet."

The widow no longer had a husband to provide for her or protect her. No inheritance had been left to her either. Step one was a hard lesson: She would find no help from man, and if not from man, where?

> *He upholds the cause of the oppressed*
> *and gives food to the hungry.*
> *The Lord sets the prisoners free,*
> *the Lord gives sight to the blind,*
> *the Lord lifts up those who are bowed down,*
> *the Lord loves the righteous.*
> Psalm 146:7–8

She stepped into the expansive court, filled with people. Some of them wore the muted browns and yellows of the common man, but many more wore fine fabrics in the beautiful blues, violets, and reds of the wealthy.

Jewels hung about the women's necks and from their wrists and ears. The men held heavy bags of silver and gold for the offering. The court was filled with the sound of donations being dropped into the shofars, and when a donation rang especially loudly, all around would turn to make note of the donors and their generous gift.

She paused for a moment and opened her hand to gaze down at the two small copper coins. With the finger of her left hand, she caressed their circumference.

The LORD watches over the foreigner
and sustains the fatherless and the widow.
PSALM 146:9

The sight of the coins in her palm was blurred by her tears of gratitude: comfort had come. Solace had found her when she reached her end and realized that it was actually no end at all, because her faithful God was there. She knew He would uphold her cause, provide for her, and sustain her.

She took a step forward and lifted her palm to the *shofar*. The two small copper coins glinted in the sunlight before falling out of sight.

They barely made a sound as they fell into the depths, and no one turned to observe her playing of the trumpet.

But nearby the Son of God had stopped everything just to watch.

Jesus called His disciples and pointed to the widow garbed in coarse goat hair among the brilliant linens and silks that others wore. Ignoring the heavy bags of gold and silver resonating loudly in the *shofarots*, Jesus focused on the soundless descent of two small copper coins. His heart was touched by her trust and profoundly moved by her adoration.

"Truly I tell you, this poor widow has put more into the treasury than all the others. They gave out of their wealth; but she, out of her poverty, put in everything—all she had to live on" (Mark 12:43–44).

Prayer

My Hope,

Still my soul. Quiet me with Your love when I am reeling from a loss, broken, and afraid. Lift my eyes to You once again, that I may remember that, though the way seems dark, all is not lost. For when I reach my end, You, my Alpha and Omega, are forever there.

I am safe in Your arms, and I adore You.

Amen

LEGION

———

The Demoniac of the Gadarenes

I took you from the ends of the earth,
*   from its farthest corners I called you.*
I said, "You are my servant";
*   I have chosen you and have not rejected you.*

ISAIAH 41:9

BEFORE YOU BEGIN, READ MATTHEW 8:28–34; MARK 5:1–20; AND LUKE 8:26–39

THE LAST RAYS OF sunlight cast long shadows across the rock-strewn floor of the cave tomb as a sobbing madman sat among the bones of the town's ancestors. He was filthy and completely naked; his body was covered with sores, scars, and patches of caked blood. He sat with his knees drawn close to his chest at the entrance of the cave, rocking back and forth. He mumbled continuously through his tears, and at times he seemed to be begging someone—or something—for mercy.

"No, no, no, no . . . Please, please, no . . ." he wailed, tugging at his matted beard and hair with long, jagged fingernails.

The wind began to howl, and below him dark clouds that obscured the sunset were rushing across the surface of the Sea of Galilee. Jagged lightning flashed between the rolling blackness and the water below. The surface of the lake that, only moments before, had been tranquil, churned as it was whipped into a fury by the driving wind.

He rocked more frantically, and his cries grew louder and louder until at last he leaped to his feet, grabbed in each hand a jagged rock from the floor of the cave, and dragged the sharp points across his chest, plowing deep gashes into his skin, gashes that quickly swelled with blood that splattered to the ground at his feet.

Then he turned his face to the darkening sky and screamed.

On the hillside below, a drove of two thousand pigs rooted and grunted, pressing into the troughs their keepers were filling with food. These Greek men had strips of cloth tied over their noses and mouths to filter the stench of the animals, but such a large herd represented great wealth, and they worked vigorously to keep the animals fed. Some of the pigs were destined for the dinner table; others would be bred. The very best of the lot would be offered to the gods as a sacrifice to invoke good fortune and fertility.

From time to time, as the wind snatched at their robes, the men glanced anxiously toward the sea and the brewing storm. Suddenly a terrifying, tormented cry split the air. They all froze, their buckets stopping in midair, and turned their eyes fearfully toward the tombs above them. Then each man frantically pled the protection of his god.

The storm intensified, bending trees low to the ground and molding ten-foot waves that it then tossed upon the shore. The herdsmen abandoned their buckets and ran for a small shelter they had crafted at the base of the hill. Little more than a crude roof held aloft by a couple of saplings, the structure did nothing to shield them from the rain that blew sideways across the plain. They hunkered low, clinging to their robes and shielding their faces from the gale. They gave up shouting to one another as the howling wind and crashing waves reached a deafening crescendo.

Then . . . all was silent.

The wind stilled, and as the herdsmen lifted their astonished faces to the sky, they saw the clouds rapidly receding. They winced and shielded their eyes from the abrupt reappearance of the brilliant setting sun. The lake before them, only moments ago a boiling tempest, was as smooth as glass, its surface broken only by the bobbing of one small boat.

The herdsmen paled with fright, finding the storm's abrupt end even more terrifying than its fury.

Dumbstruck, they stood slowly to their feet and watched the small craft row to shore in the distance. As the molten orb of the setting sun shimmered below the surface, they observed a small group of men step from the boat and haul it onto the beach.

The madman was curled up in a fetal position among the skeletons and lost in a fitful, exhausted slumber. Even in sleep, he whimpered and moaned. Then, for a moment, he was so still that he seemed to have stopped breathing, at last taking his final resting place among the dead.

Then, abruptly, his eyes flew open, and his body became rigid. A fierce grimace transformed his face into fury. He bolted upright, tilting his head from side to side as if listening for some intruder. Then, with an inhuman roar, he bolted from the cave and down the hillside toward the beach.

Jesus and His weary disciples had barely stepped onto dry land when the screaming, raging figure came hurtling toward them through the gathering darkness. Peter reached for the sword at his waist as Judas plunged his hand into his robe to grab the hilt of his dagger. All of the rest of the men scrambled for a piece of driftwood or an oar—anything they could use to defend themselves.

But not Jesus. The Messiah, His face set like stone for the battle about to begin, strode forward to meet the man. Then, with a loud voice, Jesus commanded the spirit within the demoniac to set him free.

"Come out of this man, you impure spirit!" Jesus roared (Mark 5:8).

The madman was thrown to the ground, his face landing in the sand and his arms flung wide as the demon within him began to beg. The chorus inside him screamed, vacillating between insolence and begging for mercy.

"What do you want with me, Jesus, Son of the Most High God? I beg you, don't torture me!" (Luke 8:28).

"What is your name?" Jesus asked as the demons whimpered and begged at His feet.

The demons responded with a term fit only for war.

"Legion," they replied, "for we are many" (Mark 5:9).

Yet they began to beg for mercy again. Whimpering, pleading, they searched about for any alternative to the abyss they knew awaited them. With sinister delight, their eyes focused on the herd of pigs in the distance. It was a strategic choice. Though they knew they would ultimately lose their war with the Creator, they would seize every malicious opportunity afforded them in the meantime. If they could destroy the valuable herd of pigs, the local population would be far less receptive to the Messiah. Furthermore, the fact that a running boar was the symbol for the 10th Roman Legion, Israel's oppressor, sweetened the prospect.

"If you drive us out, send us into the herd of pigs!" (Matthew 8:31).

The Savior said to them, *"Go!"* (Matthew 8:32).

The man at Jesus' feet convulsed violently. Seconds later, a loud scream rose from the herd as the pigs—shocked by the evil intrusion—leaped into the air. Terrified, they bolted and attempted to run away from the oppressive darkness that had fallen upon them.

As they stampeded down the hill, their legs pumped faster and faster. Here and there a few of the animals realized they were running out of control and attempted to stop, but to no avail. The decline was too steep and the press of the drove behind them too strong.

The thunder of their hooves and screaming filled the air as the pigs fell over one another, cascading like an avalanche headlong into the sea.

Pigs are naturally buoyant and good swimmers, but this herd was doomed by a supernatural force. The water churned as they struggled in vain to keep their heads above the surface. In a matter of moments, each one had sunk to the bottom of the Sea of Galilee, and all was quiet.

The men who had been tending the pigs stood transfixed in shock for a moment and then began to run toward the town shouting the alarm as they went.

The man at Jesus' feet rose shakily and wrapped his arms around himself in an attempt to shield his nakedness. Jesus shrugged off His outer cloak and wrapped it around the man's shoulders.

The man began weeping, voicing his gratitude over and again to the One who had set him free. Slowly, he dropped to the ground, grasped the feet of the Savior, and covered them with tears of heartfelt gratitude.

Prayer

Eternal God,

You are the Creator of the ends of the earth, and Your understanding no one can fathom.[1] You saw the morning star fall from heaven,[2] and yet, in compassion, You bend low to set me free from all that keeps me in bondage. May my moments and my days overflow with ceaseless gratitude and praise to you.

Amen

1. Isaiah 40:28
2. Isaiah 14:12

THE BETTER
CHOICE

———

In the Home of Mary and Martha

You, God, see the trouble of the afflicted;
you consider their grief and take it in hand.
The victims commit themselves to you;
you are the helper of the fatherless.

PSALM 10:14

You, LORD, hear the desire of the afflicted;
you encourage them, and you listen to their cry,
defending the fatherless and the oppressed,
so that mere earthly mortals
will never again strike terror.

PSALM 10:17–18

MARTHA KNELT BEFORE HER kneading board and punched the dough just a little too hard. *That Mary. What did she think she was doing?* Martha picked up the dough and sprinkled a little more flour on the board before tossing it back down and pummeling it again.

She let out a huff, dropped the dough into a stone bowl, and stood to her feet. She shifted the bowl to her hip and walked to the doorway where she could peer across the courtyard and into the reception room on the other side. Jesus sat teaching with His disciples gathered at His feet, and there was Mary, right in the middle of them. It was absolutely outrageous.

Martha stormed across the room to place the bowl near the oven to rise. Then she walked to a shelf full of kitchenware, reached up to the top, and pulled down a large red jug. It was wide at the bottom, with a long graceful neck and a delicate handle. She carefully placed the serving piece on a nearby stone table and began to pour olive oil into it from a larger container. The emerald-green oil flowed smoothly and filled the kitchen with a delicate aroma.

What was Mary thinking? Had she even stopped to consider the implications of her actions? By sitting at a rabbi's feet, she was assuming the position of a disciple. It was scandalous.

Martha placed the jug of olive oil on the table and started arranging dates and olives on a platter. For a woman, surviving this world meant learning how to play the game and stay in her place, which was a place of service, not at the feet of a rabbi studying theology. Of course, every little girl held stories of the great women of faith close to her heart. There was brave and beautiful Queen Esther who outwitted a powerful politician to save her people, Ruth who was faithful and courageous, and Deborah the prophetess.

But the teachings of the rabbis over the past several hundred years had done serious damage to the position of women in Israeli society. Now a woman's ideal position was at home, out of sight and quiet. She was considered inferior at best and inherently more sinful than her male counterparts at worst. Sons were preferable; daughters were a disappointment. In the words of Rabbi Ben Sirach, "Do not sit down with the women, for moth comes out of clothes, and a woman's spite out of a woman. A man's spite is preferable to a woman's kindness. Women give rise to shame and reproach" (Sirach 42:12–14).[1]

The neighbors were certainly already talking about Mary's indiscretions. Who would marry her little sister now?

Pausing, Martha looked across the courtyard again. Rabbi Jesus didn't seem to hold much respect for the traditions concerning women. He called His women followers His disciples, and He depended on them to support His ministry. He even allowed them to travel with Him! Martha loved Jesus and believed His message, but all of this radical philosophy made her more than a little nervous. Now Mary was wrapped up in it. As the older sister, Martha was responsible for Mary, so she had to do something.

Martha walked over to the oven and peered inside to check the lamb she was roasting. Then she turned, wiped her hands on a towel, and straightened her robe. She took one last look around her kitchen and marched across the courtyard.

She stood in the doorway of the reception room for a moment and waited for Jesus to notice her. Glancing up at her as He taught, He motioned to an empty spot on the floor. Martha's cheeks burned and she turned away. A few moments later, when He reached a stopping point in the discussion, He excused Himself and came to His hostess's side.

Martha set her jaw, squared her shoulders, and delivered the argument she was sure He couldn't refuse.

"Lord, don't you care that my sister has left me to do the work by myself? Tell her to help me!" (Luke 10:40).

Jesus saw straight through her protestations to the true anxieties in her heart. He saw all the wounds her society had inflicted on her spirit and all the lies she had believed about herself and her position in life. He simply loved her too much to allow her to remain in such bondage. So He held out to her a higher standard.

"Martha, Martha," the Lord answered, *"you are worried and upset about many things, but few things are needed—or indeed only one. Mary has chosen what is better, and it will not be taken away from her"* (Luke 10:41–42).

Jesus returned to His seat and resumed teaching. He had defended Mary's right to her theological studies, so with His disciples she would remain.

Martha's mind and heart were thoroughly immobilized by the expectations of her culture. It wasn't easy to reject all she had been taught from her birth until that day. But Jesus' invitation to her was a call to freedom.

The scent of roasted lamb drifted across the courtyard as Martha gazed for a moment at the empty place on the floor at Jesus' feet, an empty place that represented the better choice. It was hers to receive or reject. And Jesus would remain forever faithful in challenging Martha to embrace all God created her to be.

Prayer

My Creator,

Forgive me for holding back, embracing mediocrity, and abandoning Your glory because I am too focused on the world's expectations of me. If I am worried about pleasing others, how can I truly please You?[2] I was created for Your glory alone, O God. You deserve the best of all I am and of all I have to give.

May I never silence the song of my life, but live fearlessly, joyously, always for You.

Amen

1. Book of Sirach is one of the books in the apocrypha, a group of books included in the Catholic Bible.
2. Galatians 1:10

UNCLEAN!

———

Praise the LORD, my soul;
*   all my inmost being, praise his holy name.*
Praise the LORD, my soul,
*   and forget not all his benefits—*
who forgives all your sins
*   and heals all your diseases,*
who redeems your life from the pit
*   and crowns you with love and compassion,*
who satisfies your desires with good things
*   so that your youth is renewed like the eagle's.*
The LORD works righteousness
*   and justice for all the oppressed.*

PSALM 103:1–6

Some mornings, when I first awakened, I would think it had all been just a terrible dream. Then I would roll over and see not my wife and children on their mats beside me in the pale early light, but rows of other men. And then I would remember that nightmare and reality were one.

My roommates were a macabre sort. Their limbs were swollen, and their bodies were covered with craterlike sores, deep, red pits rimmed with scaly white flesh. The nodules that covered their foreheads, lips, and chins were like countless pebbles strewn across the sand. Every man was missing at least a couple of fingers and toes. A few wretched souls had almost none at all. Their skin, which sagged and draped limply over their gaunt faces, looked like leather. Eyes were shrunken and weak. Noses had collapsed. The men trembled in their sleep as dry coughs shook their skeletal frames. These were the outcasts of society, the living dead.

Just like me.

This reality was a horror from which I could never awaken. *I was a leper . . .*

The day that changed everything started out like any other. I rolled my mat and placed it in the corner, a task much more difficult after I lost a thumb and two fingers to injuries. I was also missing my small toe on my right foot. It is very difficult to protect fingers and toes once all sensation in them is lost. My missing nose was another story entirely. It simply seemed to collapse in on itself bit by bit. All my eyelashes had fallen out, and my eyes had become so sensitive to the sunlight that I was limited to scavenging during certain hours of the day.

That morning I slowly made my way out of the house into the early morning light. My legs were heavy, but I pushed them as fast as I could. The incessant gnawing in my empty stomach was driving my feeble body to the city gate in hopes that someone passing by would pity me and toss a piece of bread my way.

I glanced down at my feet to see blood seeping into my sandal from a sore I could not feel on the bottom of my foot. Then I heard footsteps ahead. I drew to the far edge of the road, pulled the edge of my head covering across the lower half of my face to cover my nose, and shouted the designated warning just as the travelers came into sight.

"Unclean! Unclean!"

Their revulsion was immediate and obvious. Some were horrified by my wounds. Others were terrified such a fate could befall them. The worst of all were those who snarled in contempt, confident that my affliction was an outward expression of the Lord's judgment for some secret sin. After all, wasn't leprosy called "the finger of God"?

"Bread! Bread!" I begged as the travelers hurried past. One young man paused, reached into his pack, tore off a chunk of bread, and tossed it to me before hurrying away. The bread rolled through the dust to my feet. I picked it up, quickly brushed it off, and then devoured it as I continued on my way.

After a while I grew weary of dragging my heavy legs along the road—and even wearier of the horror openly expressed by the travelers I passed. So I stopped for shelter in the shade of a rocky outcropping far enough away to no longer offend but still close enough to catch bits of the conversations that drifted to me from the road.

Over and over the travelers were excitedly discussing the same topic. The great Healer and Miracle Worker, Jesus of Nazareth, was nearby. His fame was spreading throughout all Judea. They said He healed the lame, the blind, the deaf, and the mute.

I couldn't help but think, *What if He could heal me too?* I knew, of course, that leprosy was no common illness. No one had heard of anyone being cured of leprosy in hundreds of years. As a matter of fact, it was commonly believed that healing leprosy was one of four miracles only Messiah Himself could do, and that's one reason why there was a specific temple protocol for any leper claiming to have been healed. He was required to present himself to the priests who would inspect the man's body and then investigate his claim. If the healing was found to be valid, the priests would then begin the process of confirming whether or not Messiah had indeed come at last.

As I sat in the dust, I looked down at my disfigured body and my filthy rags. I thought of my wife and children. I wondered if my mother was still living. If there were any chance I could be reunited with my family, I had to seize it. I struggled to my feet and trudged on.

"Unclean! Unclean!"

When at last I came to Jesus, a large crowd surrounded Him. I stood at a distance for a moment, my heart pounding in terror at the thought of crossing the road, breaking the law, and casting my vile decaying flesh into the midst of all that was whole and good. I took one shuddering breath and limped my way toward Him. Someone spotted me, and the cry was raised. The crowd scattered, but Jesus stood firm.

> *I threw myself face down into the dust at His feet, weeping, begging for mercy, believing the unbelievable—that He was Messiah and was therefore able to make me, even me, whole.*

"Lord, if you are willing, you can make me clean" (Luke 5:12).

Jesus did the most astonishing thing. He reached out His hand to me and *touched* me. He wasn't repulsed by my filth; He wasn't afraid of my decay.

"*I* am *willing*," he said. "*Be clean!*" (Luke 5:13).

I wish I could describe what happened next, but words fail me. There was power—great power and life-transforming love—flowing through me. Strength returned to my muscles. Feeling surged into my limbs. Fingers and toes were simply . . . restored.

I pulled back the sleeves of my robe to see perfectly smooth skin. I gingerly lifted my fingers to my face to find the nodules gone and my nose just as it should be.

I was speechless, overcome with awe and gratitude. I looked up into His kind face as tears of thankfulness streamed down my cheeks.

Then He said to me, *"Don't tell anyone, but go, show yourself to the priest and offer the sacrifices that Moses commanded for your cleansing, as a testimony to them"* (Luke 5:14).

And I rose to make my way to the temple in Jerusalem. I was unclean no more.

Prayer

My God,

The world is fraught with suffering. Be near today to those who are outcast and in desperate poverty. Give me ears to hear their cries and an open hand to help meet their needs. Break my heart, Jesus, for those for whom Your heart breaks, that I may extend mercy to the untouchables and receive the forgotten as Your dear children.

Amen

Jesus Walks on Water

———

He reached down from on high and took hold of me;
*   he drew me out of deep waters.*
He rescued me from my powerful enemy,
*   from my foes, who were too strong for me.*
They confronted me in the day of my disaster,
*   but the Lord was my support.*
He brought me out into a spacious place;
*   he rescued me because he delighted in me.*

2 Samuel 22:17–20

Thomas sat down with a thud next to the first pair of oars as Judas threw a coil of rope into the bottom of the boat with far more force than was necessary.

"We are leaving? Now?" he asked incredulously.

"That's what He says," Peter responded grimly.

"Well, where is He? What's He doing?" Judas demanded.

"He is dismissing the crowd, and then He said He is going up on the mountaintop to pray. Alone," Peter answered.

"But why now?" Thomas countered. "He just fed that entire crowd from a few little sardines and a couple of barley loaves. It was just like when God fed our fathers with manna in the wilderness. Did you hear the crowd? They are ready to make Him king! He has the will of the people behind Him."

"Then this is the moment to rally them, to form an army and drive Rome from our inheritance," Judas claimed.

"He said to get in the boat and meet Him on the other side. So that is what we are going to do," Peter said.

The men unhappily took their places in the boat. Peter put one foot on the dock and shoved off from shore as he watched Jesus ascend the side of the mountain and the crowd slip away. He shook his head and sat down at the steering oars.

When Jesus finally lifted His head from prayer, the night was long spent and the morning near. He stood on the side of the mountain and turned toward the Sea of Galilee. A strong breeze blew from the water, tugged at His robe and pushed His hair back from His face. A bright moon hung over the surface of the lake, shining a silvery spotlight on the little boat below.

He watched as it rocked back and forth. The sail was tethered to the mast, and the men strained at the oars as a fierce wind pushed against them and thwarted their attempts to reach the opposite shore. He frowned as He watched their struggle. They should have made it to land long ago. They were definitely in trouble.

And the disciples knew it.

Every thought of kings and kingdoms had been washed away in their struggle against wind and waves.

Over and again the disciples leaned forward and pulled against the oars until pain seared their backs and their arms and legs trembled with the effort. Sweat dripped from their brows and into their eyes as their hearts pounded and chests heaved with their work. Four of them could row at a time with a fifth man at the steering oar. They took turns at the brutal, seemingly endless labor in an effort to provide each man a little relief.

"Come on, Peter. It is your turn for a break," James said, motioning for Peter to relinquish his oar.

Peter gratefully collapsed in the floor of the boat, hung his head, and gasped for breath. Then he lifted his eyes to the far shore to gauge their progress.

"Well?" John asked. "How are we doing?"

Peter shook his head. "We are no closer."

John clenched his teeth in determination as he struggled with his oar.

Moments later, Peter watched as John's eyes widened. John gasped, shook his head, squeezed his eyes tightly shut, and then opened them wide again. He leaned forward and stared past Peter into the dark waters behind him.

"John? What's wrong?" Peter asked as he turned around to look behind him.

There, gliding along on the surface of the water, a figure was moving toward them in the moonlight. Peter scrambled backward as the cries of the other men erupted all around him. They had spotted the apparition as well.

Then the familiar voice of Jesus rang out across the water. *"Take courage! It is I. Don't be afraid"* (Matthew 14:27).

Peter crept toward the side of the boat and called back to Him. "Lord, if it is you, tell me to come to you on the water."

"Come," Jesus replied (Matthew 14:28–29).

Peter sat on the edge of the boat as the wind whipped his robe and the waves splashed over his feet. He looked down at the churning waters and then up again at Jesus. Peter closed his eyes, took a deep breath, and . . . stood. When the disciples yelled out cries of amazement that rose above the wind, Peter opened his eyes and laughed in wonder. He looked up to find Jesus waiting for him with an outstretched hand. Peter took another deep breath and then a step, and then another, and another.

Suddenly, a huge gust of wind bore down on Peter, and he involuntarily looked from the eyes of Jesus to the threat around him. Above him clouds rolled by as the wind whipped the sea into waves and crashing whitecaps. His mouth and throat went dry, and his heart began pounding in his ears. As the water gave way beneath him, he began to sink beneath the cold, gray surface of the stormy lake.

Panicked, he turned to Jesus. "Lord, save me!"

Jesus reached out instantly, took Peter by the hand, and lifted him above the waves once again. Seconds later, both were in the boat, the wind slowed to a whisper, and the surface of the lake grew calm.

Jesus looked around at His exhausted disciples who stared at Him in awe. Then, one by one, they dropped to their knees in the floor of the boat, bowed down before Jesus, and cried out over and again.

"Truly you are the Son of God" (Matthew 14:33).

Only hours before, Jesus had crushed their Messianic hopes when He'd sent the crowd away. For so long, they had mourned for Israel's freedom, *longed* for the day Messiah would come and God would deliver His children from the cruel oppression of Rome by His mighty hand. The disciples' disappointment, the wind, and the waves had been gifts in disguise. They were tools in the Father's loving hands used to deliver them from their temporal hope of an earthly ruler to a more enduring kingdom. Jesus was King of the wind and the waves, the moon and the stars, the sun overhead and the stones beneath their feet. He was Israel's *eternal* Messianic hope, the King of glory.

And He is an eternal King whose eye is always on His children and whose heart is forever moved with compassion for those in need. This King moves heaven and earth and walks upon the waves to come to their rescue.

Prayer _____

Eternal King,

Deliver me from earthly ambitions and temporal affections. Grant me the faith to trust the path You have ordained for me, even when it is marked with seemingly impossible circumstances. I find myself hesitant at the altar of surrender, Jesus, afraid of losing all I hold dear. Help me to remember that Your love for me is completely and forever good. Truly, nothing I hold precious is secure until I release it into Your loving hands.

Amen

Upon This Rock

Peter's Confession

Listen, you heavens, and I will speak;
    hear, you earth, the words of my mouth.
Let my teaching fall like rain
    and my words descend like dew,
like showers on new grass,
    like abundant rain on tender plants.
I will proclaim the name of the LORD.
    Oh, praise the greatness of our God!
He is the Rock, his works are perfect,
    and all his ways are just.
A faithful God who does no wrong,
    upright and just is he.

DEUTERONOMY 32:1–4

Before you begin, read Matthew 16:13–19
and Mark 8:27–30

The disciples were unusually quiet on this beautiful and clear morning. The Roman road beneath their sandals eased their traveling, and the scenery that stretched in every direction was verdant and beautiful. Fig trees, laden with honeyed fruit, grew tall and broad. Mighty sycamores, their trunks draped with lush vines, shaded the path. Nearby, oleander and wild roses flanked the banks of a rushing stream. The cool morning air was sweetly perfumed with honeysuckle.

This was the land of God's bounteous promise to Israel. The soil had been made abundantly fertile by steady rainfall and ancient volcanic eruptions. It was a land of fruit, oil, and honey; golden with wheat, leaping with fat lambs, and flowing with the richest wine. This was ancient Bashan,* picture of God's richest blessing, and illustration of His most fervent warning.

In his last address to the Israelites, Moses had prophesied that despite God's generosity, His children would turn from Him, rejecting their "Rock."

> *Jeshurun grew fat and kicked;*
> *filled with food, they became heavy and sleek.*
> *They abandoned the God who made them*
> *and rejected the Rock their Savior.*
> Deuteronomy 32:15

Now Moses' words and warnings rang in the disciples' hearts and minds as each step they took carried them farther and farther away from observant Judaism and into a land where no upright Jewish man would venture. This region was such the antithesis of all that the Jews deemed right and good that it had earned the moniker "the other side." It was not only on the other side of the Sea of Galilee geographically from the disciples' homes, but it was the other side socially, religiously, and morally from the Jewish ideal. The disciples were following Jesus deep into enemy territory where the Law had been lost, swallowed whole by Hellenism. Here, the worship of the One True God had been exchanged for gods of wood and stone. Bashan did, indeed, forget the God who had so richly blessed her. She was now Caesarea Philippi, and her heart pulsed with idolatry.

At a sharp turn in the road, the city was suddenly before them, nestled at the base of massive Mount Hermon.

Jesus motioned to a quiet spot beneath an outcropping of trees where, in view of the city, He could teach His disciples.

And these men grew even more sober as they stared at the scene before them. There, on the side of the mountain, was an elaborate worship site towering over Caesarea Philippi on an almost three-hundred-foot natural terrace. The western end of the terrace was anchored by a yawning cave revered as a grotto to the god Pan since the arrival of the Greeks.

Shepherds had long come to this site to worship their patron god both in the grotto and at the spring at its base. Herod the Great, however, had taken idolatrous worship at the site to a new level. Now, a gleaming white, columned temple towered in front of the cavern. It was the Temple of Zeus,* built in honor of Herod's patron, Caesar Augustus.

The majestic temple was built without a back wall so that worshippers could directly enter the sacred grotto. These were the gates of Hades, believed to be the entrance to the underworld. The cave at the rear contained a still and unfathomably deep pool where unfortunate souls may have been thrown as sacrifices to the gods of the underworld.

Jesus turned to His disciples.

"Who do people say I am?" (Mark 8:27).

The answers rang out.

"John the Baptist."

"Elijah."

"Jeremiah or one of the prophets."

These were the answers of the masses, of those who had come to hear Jesus speak or witness His miracles. But what about these men, with Him now, who had walked with Him and lived alongside Him for so long? Their time together was growing short. Had they not yet grown enough to discover the truth?

"But what about you?" Jesus asked them. *"Who do you say that I am?"* (Matthew 16:15).

Simon Peter's voice rang out sure and clear: "You are the Messiah, the Son of the living God."

"Blessed are you, Simon Son of Jonah, for this was not revealed to you by flesh and blood, but by my Father in heaven. And I tell you that you are Peter, and on this rock I will build my church, and the gates of Hades will not overcome it" (Matthew 16:16–18).

―――――――――

Jesus had changed Simon's name to *Peter*, "the rock." Now his very name would remind the disciples not only of that place but also of that day when their Master pointed them back to their history and prepared them for their future. Just as God, the Rock, brought Israel to Bashan and blessed her . . . only to suffer her rejection, so Jesus had come to redeem His people—and He would suffer great rejection in the days ahead. Oh, how the disciples would need to be reminded of the unwavering faithfulness of God, their Rock, in the days to come.

From Caesarea Philippi, they would turn to Jerusalem. The time had come for Jesus to fulfill His ultimate destiny as Redeemer of all mankind by surrendering Himself to the unspeakable brutality of a Roman cross. What horrors the disciples would witness! How their hopes and dreams would be devastated! And Peter would also bear the terrible, crushing guilt of betraying his Lord. But Jesus, in His great mercy, had launched a preemptive strike of hope by changing His beloved disciple's very name into a reminder of God's goodness, strength, and deliverance.

The lesson was over: the seed of hope had been planted, and the Messianic declaration delivered. It was time to head back home. It was time for Jesus to begin the last stage of His journey to the cross.

Prayer

My Rock,

You are forever faithful. Help me to remember that though the forces of evil rage in these last days, the ultimate victory is already won. Grant me the grace to live courageously in this truth and to remember that no matter how dark the moments before me seem, You—the Light of this world, the Light of truth and hope, of power and goodness— have promised to prevail.

Amen

BARTIMAEUS

In that day the deaf will hear the words of the scroll,
and out of gloom and darkness
the eyes of the blind will see.

ISAIAH 29:18

HE HAD SEEN MANY things in his life. He had seen the long shadows, cast by the setting sun, darken the walls of Herod's magnificent winter palace. He had seen the sun rise, bathing the verdant plain of the Jordan in hues of crimson and gold. He had witnessed the processions of the wealthy and powerful as they made their way down the streets of Jericho. He had seen dark, rich wine flow into his glass, fresh bread come out of the oven, children playing tag in the streets, and the smiles of those he loved.

He had even witnessed the extraction of the miracle plant opobalsamum.* An incision was made in the bark to free the sap, glutinous and milky white. The sap was carefully collected, for it was precious. Once it was allowed to sit for a while, it hardened into a creamy balm reputed to cure a myriad of infirmities—everything from headaches to urinary tract infections. Some even said it had the power to restore sight.

Bartimaeus laughed bitterly as he smoothed his cloak on the ground beneath him.

"Well, not for everyone, I guess."

When he first lost his sight, he dwelled almost continually on such things. It was incredibly difficult to accept that he had somehow gone from being a productive member of Jordanian society to a beggar on the street. After a while the hunger in his stomach overcame the pride in his heart, and he spread his cloak on a busy street, raised his milky, sightless eyes to the crowds passing by, and lifted his voice and upturned palm.

"Give to God!" he shouted over and again. When, at last, someone tossed a coin his way, he stood to loudly proclaim their generosity and nobility. It was, after all, a beggar's duty.

He was shy at first, but in time he became more assertive. He also learned quickly that it was important to move to wherever the crowds were, and that strategy required listening attentively to the conversations that drifted by him. If a visiting ruler was coming to town for a little respite, for instance, Bartimaeus would spread his cloak near Herod's winter palace complex.* On market day, Bartimaeus stationed himself near the money changers. When the time drew near for the festivals, he always placed his cloak under a palm tree by the side of the road near Jericho's gate so he could intercept the pilgrims as they passed through the city on their way to Jerusalem.

Bartimaeus found it was amazing how much he could learn just by listening. Much of what he heard was useless gossip, but occasionally something of real interest drifted his way.

Lately, he had been hearing talk of a Prophet who taught with great authority and performed mighty works.

It was said He could cast out demons, raise the dead, heal lepers, and cause the lame to walk again. He had even heard that this Man could restore sight to the blind.

Daily, there were debates about Him in the streets. Some said He was a good man; others declared Him to be of the devil. There were even those who dared ask if the Son of David, the Messiah, had come at last.

Bartimaeus had time to think about all of these things and come to his own conclusions . . . and fuel his own hopes.

"Give to God!"

Hand outstretched, palm raised, and another coin received.

He delivered the expected oration of praise, dropped the alms onto the small pile at the corner of his cloak, and waited for the next pilgrim.

Suddenly, he heard the sound of a large crowd coming his way. The sandals of the masses stirred up dust that coated his hair and beard and filled his nose and mouth. He scooted to one corner of his cloak and drew the opposite end up over the bottom of his face to filter the grime.

He dropped the cloak slightly in order to call out to the crowd.

"What is happening?"

He reached out to tug at the robes swishing by, trying to get someone to pay attention to him.

"Excuse me! What is all of the commotion? What is happening?"

At last a woman paused to tell him.

"It is Jesus of Nazareth. He is here!"

Desperation is a great giver of clarity: Bartimaeus needed no time to decide what to do next.

"Jesus! Son of David!" he shouted. "Have mercy on me!" (Mark 10:47).

The crowd turned to him in disgust.

"Shut your mouth, son of filth!"[1]

But Bartimaeus knew what it meant to be despised. He also knew that the chance of a lifetime was literally passing him by, so he called to the Savior all the louder.

"Son of David! Have mercy on me!"

The pitiful cry of the beggar drifted across the
multitude to the Healer's ears, and He stood still.

"Son of David! Have mercy!"

Jesus turned to the crowd. *"Call him"* (Mark 10:49).

Bartimaeus heard the crowd settle down, and then a ripple of voices floated across the surface to him. Suddenly someone near him said, "Cheer up! On your feet! He's calling you!"

Bartimaeus leaped to his feet and threw his cloak away from him. Alms took flight and scattered in the dust as the afternoon sun glinted off their surfaces.

The blind man reached out, and a strong hand grasped his own and began leading him through the mass of bodies. At last, he reached the center and stopped.

Jesus spoke tenderly to him.

"*What do you want me to do for you?*"

"Rabbi," Bartimaeus responded with a quivering voice. "I want to see."

Jesus placed His fingertips gently on Bartimaeus's eyelids.

"*Go,*" He said, "*your faith has healed you*" (Mark 10:51–52).

Jesus lowered His hands, and Bartimaeus slowly opened his eyes to brilliant sunlight and the smiling face of the Savior. Bartimaeus laughed in wonder, raised his fists to heaven, and shouted, "Hallelujah! Hallelujah! God has healed me! I was blind but now I see!"

Jesus laughed with delight as a roar of praise exploded from the crowd.

But it was time to move on . . . Jerusalem and Jesus' ultimate destiny awaited Him.

And Bartimaeus would follow Him to the holy city, glorifying God all along the way.

Prayer

My Healer,

I have listened to lies, O Son of David, lies about who I am and what I am worth until my vision has been darkened to all I was created to be. Shine the light of truth into my mind and heart where the lies of the enemy have held sway for too long. I long to be fully awake, fully alive . . . for the glory of God.

Amen

1. Bartimaeus means "son of filth" or "the unclean"

LAZARUS

I will deliver this people from the power of the grave;
I will redeem them from death.
Where, O death, are your plagues?
Where, O grave, is your destruction?

HOSEA 13:14

MARY'S EYES SHOT OPEN in the dark. She lay on her mat for a moment trying to determine what had awakened her when she heard a high-pitched wheeze pierce the stillness. It was coming from Lazarus's room. Quietly she reached for a nearby lamp, lit it, then tiptoed past sleeping Martha to go to her brother.

She stood in his doorway for a moment just listening. Not feeling well that evening, he had gone to bed early. She was anxious about him now but hesitated to awaken him if he were actually resting. Another wheeze broke the silence again.

"Lazarus," she called into the darkness. There was no answer. Cautiously, she crossed the dark room to kneel by his mat and then held the lamp aloft so that she might see him better. He tossed fitfully in his sleep. He was pale, and his hair clung to the sides of his face, soaked with sweat. She lay her left palm across his forehead and found it blistering hot. His chest rose and fell rapidly in shallow breaths.

Mary's heart began to pound in fear.

"Lazarus! Lazarus!" she called, shaking him gently by the shoulder, but he just tossed his head side to side, incoherent, unable to respond. Mary had seen enough illnesses in her time to know there was only one hope for her brother—and there was no time to waste.

In a heartbeat she was at Martha's side shaking her awake.

"Martha, it is Lazarus. He is very sick. The sun is almost up. Go next door and find someone who is willing to go to the Jordan valley and find the Teacher. When He hears His friend is sick, He will come. I know He can heal our brother. Hurry!"

The message was delivered and the sisters waited. They knelt by Lazarus's mat and prayed. They bathed his forehead with cool cloths and dripped water between his parched lips. Hour by hour, they watched as his breathing became weaker. As days passed, they held onto hope only to have it fade away. Then Mary and Martha watched their brother die.

Relatives and mourners came. The body was washed, wrapped in spices and linens, and placed in a tomb. A stone was pushed over the entrance, and the sisters went home to grieve.

The Teacher still had not come.

It was said that until the fourth day after death, the soul lingered near the body, and decomposition began only after the soul departed. Perhaps the tiniest glimmer of hope remained in the sisters' hearts until then. Yet with the dawning of that fourth hopeless day, after all was lost, Martha received word that the Teacher was just outside Bethany.

Wearily, she rose from her seat, smoothed the creases from the lap of her robe, and began walking toward the edge of town to meet Him.

When she saw Him in the distance, tears began to fill her eyes and then stream down her cheeks. She had witnessed the impossible from Him time and again, convincing her beyond all doubt that He was from God. Until now. He had failed her when she needed Him most. Her heart was shattered; her faith was worn thin.

In a moment, He was before her. She swallowed hard and looked into His eyes. It was much too late for pleasantries. She had nothing left for it.

> *"Lord," Martha said to Jesus, "if you had been here,*
> *my brother would not have died. But I know that*
> *even now God will give you whatever you ask."*

Did she? Had Martha dreamed big enough dreams?
Jesus said to her, *"Your brother will rise again."*

Ever-pragmatic, she answered, "I know he will rise again in the resurrection at the last day."

Jesus said to her, *"I am the resurrection and the life. The one who believes in me will live, even though they die; and whoever lives by believing in me will never die. Do you believe this?"*

"Yes, Lord," she replied, "I believe you are the Messiah, the Son of God, who is to come into the world" (John 11:23–27).

And with that, she turned from Him and went home to get Mary.

Mary was sitting on a low stool surrounded by mourners. She was staring off into space, her eyes rimmed red from weeping. Martha walked over and held out her hand to her sister. Mary took it and Martha led her to a quiet corner where they could have some privacy.

She paused for a moment, held her sister's hands in her own, and then spoke gently to her.

"The Teacher is here," she said, "and is asking for you."

Mary's face contorted with grief, and then she turned to slip out the front door. She ran through the village streets, her vision blurred with tears, as Martha and a growing crowd of spectators followed her. When she found Jesus outside the city where Martha had left Him, she fell at His feet, sobbing.

"Lord, if you had been here, my brother would not have died!" (John 11:32).

Broken, she lay in the dust and wailed. She held nothing back as she poured out the full torrent of her grief at His feet.

Jesus looked at Mary and the crowd that had followed her. They were weeping as well, and His heart was gripped with sorrow for them.

"Where have you laid him?" Jesus asked through His own tears (John 11:34).

They led the Teacher to the grave. The tomb had been fashioned out of a cave. A stairway, hewn into the side of it, descended into its depths. Lazarus's body lay on one of the benches that had been carved out of the cave's rock walls. At street level above, a large rock had been placed over the entrance.

"*Take away the stone,*" Jesus said (John 11:39).

Horrified, Martha left Mary's side and rushed forward.

"But, Lord," she said, "by this time there is a bad odor, for he has been there four days" (John 11:39).

She knew Jesus had raised the dead before, but it had always been soon after the person's death. No one had ever raised a dead man four days after death. How could that happen?

Jesus turned to her and said, "*Did I not tell you that if you believe, you will see the glory of God?*" (John 11:40).

Martha paused for a moment and then motioned to some men nearby to move the stone. Instinctively, the crowd protectively lifted the sleeves of their robes to cover their noses and mouths.

Jesus looked to heaven and prayed.

"*Father, I thank you that you have heard me. I knew that you always hear me, but I said this for the benefit of the people standing here, that they may believe that you sent me*" (John 11:41–42).

Then Jesus took a deep breath and *shouted.*

"*Lazarus, come out!*" (John 11:43).

Breathless silence fell over the crowd. A faint rustling came from within the tomb, and a moment later a hand that had been wrapped in linen reached up over the top step. Lazarus crawled out of his tomb and into the brilliant sunlight. Still wrapped head to toe in burial cloths, he was miraculously alive!

It was something only Messiah could have done—and that truth was not lost on the crowd that had erupted in joyous cheering.

A broad smile lit Jesus' face as He watched His friend struggle clumsily against His now unnecessary wrappings.

Jesus turned to the crowd and said, *"Take off the grave clothes and let him go"* (John 11:44).

Prayer

My Comforter,

When I have prayed countless prayers, believed through the darkest nights, and waited long for Your deliverance only to find all that is most precious to me in pieces at me feet, hold me near. Remember, gentle Lamb of God, that I am but dust, a frail thing of earth. When I can go no farther, renew my faith in the hope that although this world may be full of trouble, You have overcome it,[1] that although weeping lasts for the night, joy comes in the morning.[2]

Come quickly, Lord Jesus.

Amen

1. John 16:33
2. Psalm 30:5

"O Jerusalem"

———

The stone the builders rejected
    has become the cornerstone;
the Lord has done this,
    and it is marvelous in our eyes.
The Lord has done it this very day;
    let us rejoice today and be glad.
Lord, save us!
    Lord, grant us success!
Blessed is he who comes in the name of the Lord.

Psalm 118:22–26

THE NEWS RIPPLED THROUGH the temple courts crowded with Passover pilgrims.

"He raised him from the dead . . ."

"Four days in the tomb! Four days!"

"Just outside of Jerusalem, in Bethany . . ."

"Lazarus. I was there. I saw it with my own eyes . . ."

"Only Messiah could do such wonders . . ."

"Messiah, come at last . . ."

"His name is Jesus, and He is on His way here now. The whole city is going out to meet Him. Hurry!"

The worshippers were seized by Messianic hope. They surged out of the temple courts toward the Mount of Olives.* With each step they took toward their King, the story was told and retold, and their numbers grew. As they went along, the joyful procession cut palm branches, a symbol of Israeli nationalism and independence. Jesus was just outside the city limits in Bethphage,* and they would give this King a proper welcome.

Jesus had left the home of His dear friends Lazarus, Mary, and Martha for the last time and begun the twenty-minute uphill walk toward Bethphage where two of His disciples awaited His arrival. He had sent them ahead to acquire His kingly mount for His entry into Jerusalem.

The road between Bethany and Bethphage was a wide mountain path strewn with rock and loose stones. It rose steeply, a rough ribbon bordering a fir-lined hillside on its right, with a sheer drop-off on the left. When Jesus arrived in Bethphage, the most strenuous part of His journey was already over. From there He would ride a donkey down the Mount of Olives and into

Jerusalem, not for convenience but to fulfill a Messianic prophesy made by Zechariah centuries earlier:

> *Rejoice greatly, Daughter Zion!*
> *Shout, Daughter Jerusalem!*
> *See, your king comes to you,*
> *righteous and victorious,*
> *lowly and riding on a donkey,*
> *on a colt, the foal of a donkey.*
> ZECHARIAH 9:9

Long ago, during the years of Israel's united kingdom, Solomon had ridden a mule to the Gihon Spring to be anointed king. Jesus would enter Jerusalem on a donkey. The people would not miss the significance of His choice.

Even so, a donkey might not fit the image of the kind of king the Jewish people wanted. They longed for a conquering hero who would send Rome running and return Israel to her former glory. In their mind, a war-horse would be more appropriate. But Jesus was a different kind of king, and His kingdom, alien to all they could imagine. This King would enter Jerusalem humbly as a gentle Prince of Peace.

As planned, the two disciples Jesus had sent ahead met Him in Bethphage with the donkey, but they were not alone. A large crowd of joyous Passover pilgrims accompanied them. When they saw Jesus, they began shouting praises and waving palm branches. As Jesus mounted the donkey and began His descent, the crowd lined the road. Many of them removed their cloaks and spread them on the ground in front of Him, proclaiming Him their Messiah.

"Hosanna!"

"Blessed is he who comes in the name of the Lord!"

"Blessed is the coming kingdom of our father David!"

"Hosanna in the highest heaven!" (Mark 11:9–10).

The shouts of the crowd continued as Jesus made His way over the ridge of the mountain. A moment later, Jerusalem first came into view. The wealth of the city was displayed upon her terraces, rising ever upward in magnificence. The beautiful Maccabean palace* was flanked by the elaborate homes of the high priests, but none compared to Herod the Great's palace, mounted on the summit and awash in marble, lush gardens, and refreshing pools. The home boasted vast halls, Roman baths, and elegantly decorated bedchambers where the Roman procurator Pontius Pilate rested whenever he was in Jerusalem.

The road before Jesus descended slightly. Moments later, it rose again steeply once more before reaching a level stretch of rock, and instantly the entire city came into view. Jerusalem glittered like jewels in the afternoon sun. The temple shone in gold and marble in the center on an expansive thirty-five-acre man-made platform, edged by glorious palaces and luxurious estates that gently gave way to the suburbs on the city's slopes. Lush gardens and fragrant fruit orchards, scattered like emeralds in her midst, embellished her borders. Countless olive trees—ancient, gnarled, and majestic—graced her hills.

A vast white wave crested the hills to the left of Jerusalem as shepherds led temple sheep toward the city gates. Thousands of them would be offered in sacrifice during the coming week's Passover celebration.

Beautiful Jerusalem, City of David, Crown of Israel . . .

> *Jesus gazed upon her walls and pools, her prosperity and peace, and in an instant the scene before Him changed.*

Through His divine foresight, God allowed another image to enter the present.

Looking at Jerusalem's future, Jesus saw Roman troops, thirsty for blood and temple gold, encircling her in a lethal snare. He listened to every tree groan and fall as the Roman army moved toward Jerusalem's gates. Like a great cloud of locusts, that army consumed all living things in order to construct the embankments that would surround the city.

Jesus listened to the terrifying roar of the siege engines as the Roman soldiers hurled seventy-five-pound stones over the city's walls. There were deafening crashes and screams of agony and terror as the missiles found their marks.

The Son of David peered through the walls of Jerusalem under siege and saw the fingerprints of famine: His children were withered to skin and bone, their abdomens swollen with want.

He saw them lift leather belts and sandals to their lips, and even strip the trim from their shields to consume it in their desperate hunger. Jesus watched famine stalk His children until their fallen bodies were piled in the streets.

Survivors were so desperate that they began to risk slipping through the walls to forage for wild plants and herbs. More often than not, the Romans captured them. After torturing these desperate Jews, the Romans crucified them in front of the city walls, as many as five hundred each day.

Jesus witnessed the breaching of the walls at last. He saw the enraged Roman soldiers surge into the city, slaughtering everyone in their path—men, women, and children, all unarmed and helpless, all weakened by starvation.

Then a Roman soldier grasped a torch and stood on the shoulders of a comrade to toss the flaming brand into a low, golden window of the temple sanctuary. The people cried out in dismay and threw themselves upon the temple steps in an attempt to save it. Their devotion only seemed to enrage their oppressors even more. The Romans slaughtered them and piled the bodies higher and higher around the altar.

Blood and fire raced through the streets of Jerusalem as infants were thrown from her walls and the words of Psalm 79 echoed through every mourning heart.

> *O God, the nations have invaded your inheritance;*
>   *they have defiled your holy temple,*
>   *they have reduced Jerusalem to rubble. . . .*
> *They have poured out blood like water*
>   *all around Jerusalem,*
>   *and there is no one to bury the dead.*
>   PSALM 79:1, 3

Jesus, surrounded by joyous pilgrims proclaiming Him king, looked into the future and saw the destruction to come. Overcome with sorrow, He lifted his face to heaven and wailed.[1]

O, Jerusalem . . .

"If you, even you, had only known on this day what would bring you peace— but now it is hidden from your eyes. The days will come upon you when your enemies will build an embankment against you and encircle you and hem you in on every side. They will dash you to the ground, you and the children within your walls. They will not leave one stone on another, because you did not rec- ognize the time of God's coming to you." (Luke 19:42–44)

As the donkey advanced, the pilgrims continued to shout their praises, welcoming their king, as He entered His holy city not on a warhorse, but on a donkey. They had visions of a kingdom they dreamed of for Him, for *themselves*. Their demand for a kingdom of their own design would blind them to the truth—the truth that Jesus would redeem them from the kingdom of sin and death by abandoning Himself to the brutality of sinful men. He would conquer through His death.

And as they exulted, the King's face alone was wet with tears.

Prayer

My King,

How wondrous is Your heart—forever longing for me in spite of my rebellion and my relentless forgetfulness of You. Remind me today to relinquish my demands for an earthly kingdom built according to my own desires and to choose You above all. Give me greater love for You, for You alone are worthy.

Amen

1. "The contrast was, indeed, terrible between the Jerusalem that rose before Him in all its beauty, glory, and security, and the Jerusalem which he saw in vision dimly rising on the sky, with the camp of the enemy around about it on every side, hugging it close and closer in deadly embrace, and the very 'stockade' which the Roman Legions raised around it; then, another scene in the shifting panorama, and the city laid with the ground, and the gory bodies of her children among her ruins; and yet another scene: the silence and desolateness of death by the Hand of God—not one stone left upon another!" Alfred Edersheim, *The Life and Times of Jesus the Messiah*, New York, Longmans, Green, and Co., 1897, pg. 329.

THE KINGDOM OF GOD

Washing the Disciples' Feet

Seek the LORD while he may be found;
  call on him while he is near.
Let the wicked forsake their ways
  and the unrighteous their thoughts.
Let him turn to the LORD, and he will have mercy on them,
  and to our God, for he will freely pardon.

"For my thoughts are not your thoughts,
  neither are your ways my ways,"
  declares the LORD.
"As the heavens are higher than the earth,
  so are my ways higher than your ways
  and my thoughts than your thoughts."

ISAIAH 55:6–9

PETER SHIFTED THE WEIGHT of the lamb on his shoulders just a little bit.

"Do you want me to carry it for a while?" John asked.

"No, I have it. I just want to hurry and get there so that we can be in the first group of sacrifices."

John turned and scanned the crowd of jubilant worshippers who were making their way to the temple, and then he strained to see how much distance they had left to cover.

"I think we will make it. We are almost there."

Soon they were filing into the expansive temple courts and moving toward the massive bronze Nicanor Gates. For the moment the gates stood open, but they would close at the time of sacrifice. Peter and John took their places in line among the first division of worshippers. Before them stretched two long lines of priests and Levites, dressed in white; all twenty-four courses* were called to duty. From the time of Moses, the priesthood had been divided into courses which would rotate in their various duties of service at the Temple. On this special day, every priest would serve during the Passover celebration. The priests would perform their sacrificial duties with almost industrial efficiency, for on this day the blood of thousands of lambs would flow in the temple courts.

The crowd stilled as the Gates of Nicanor began to groan closed and three long blasts sounded from a silver trumpet, signaling that the moment for the sacrifice had come.

In response to this cue, Peter stilled the lamb at his feet and pulled its head back as John slit its throat. The priest in front of them caught the blood of the lamb in a golden bowl and passed it to the priest next to him, who in turn gave him an empty bowl for the next sacrifice. The blood of the lamb then joined the blood of countless others as it was poured over the altar.

Next, the lamb was prepared for the sacrifice. The priests flayed and cleaned the animal before they slit open the abdomen to remove the fatty portions that were to be offered on the altar. Finally, the priests returned the prepared lamb to be carried on a stave between the two men. Before the next division of sacrifices was even completed, Peter and John were on their way back to the Upper Room to finish preparing the meal.

They wound their way through crowded Jerusalem, up and down the hilly cobblestone streets, until they came to the home where the feast would be held. The disciple who lived there had provided the best room for them, the Upper Room, as well as all the other supplies for the meal. They took the sacrifice into the courtyard where an oven awaited them. John started the fire as Peter prepared the lamb according to the Passover restrictions. He sharpened a pomegranate stake and skewered the lamb whole from the mouth to vent and then hung it over the fire to roast, careful to be sure that no part of it touched the sides of the oven so that it might be presented undefiled. Not one bone was to be broken.

While the lamb roasted, the men climbed the outer staircase to the Upper Room to set the table. They carried a large amphora of wine between them as they went. Wine, which represented joy, would flow freely at the Paschal* supper. In fact, each participant was expected to drink at least four cups.

Once on the roof, Peter and John ducked into the shady sanctuary of the Upper Room and carefully placed the amphora against the wall. John surveyed the room for a moment, and then he walked over to a nearby shelf and began to take down stone plates, cups, and bowls for the triclinium table. This low table and its surrounding couches were essential for the celebration. Tradition mandated that those feasting were to do so reclining as a symbol of their freedom, for a slave eats standing while his master rests.

In the meantime, Peter had gone back downstairs and returned with three large loaves of bread and a basket of bitter herbs. Leavened bread was always a central part of every meal, but on this night the bread would remain unleavened, symbolizing the haste with which their fathers left Egypt.

Peter placed the loaves of bread on the table and then began to pull endive, lettuce, and beets from the basket to fill the bowls. John carefully filled small bowls nearby with water, vinegar, salt, and *charoseth*, a paste made of ground almonds, raisins, dates, and vinegar. As they dipped the herbs into these condiments and ate them during the feast, they would be reminded of the bitterness of their slavery in Egypt.

Long shadows began to fall onto the table as the setting sun prompted Peter and John to return to the courtyard to retrieve the lamb. The lamb, of course, would be the central dish. Its presence on the Paschal table was a poignant reminder of God's grace in Egypt as He passed over the blood-sprinkled doorways of the Israelites on the night of their deliverance. The two men placed the roasted lamb on a platter and carried it between them up the stairs to its position of honor in the center of the table. John ducked out of the room for a moment and came back carrying two lamps. Together, they worked their way around the room, using the lamps to light the oil lamps that rested in niches in the walls. Just as the last lamp was lit, there was the sound of footsteps on the stairs outside. The rest of their group had arrived.

Jesus entered first and came to greet both Peter and John. Silence fell over the men, for as the host, Jesus would assign seats around the table. As the leader, Jesus would automatically take the second seat. He motioned for John to take the first.

Peter stood a little straighter. Since John was given the first seat, then surely he would be given the seat of honor to Jesus' left. But Jesus motioned to Judas to take that place. One by one, each disciple was assigned his position as Peter waited, cheeks burning, until there was only one seat left . . . the servant's seat.

Peter couldn't believe it. Wasn't he the one who had confessed Jesus as the Messiah at Caesarea Philippi? Didn't Jesus in return ordain him into his rabbinical authority afterward? What is more, Peter had worked beside John all day preparing for the meal. Why should he be sent to the servant's seat?

His thoughts were interrupted by the hush that fell over the group as Jesus raised the first glass of wine and began to pronounce the blessing over it.

"Blessed are you, Jehovah our God, Who has created the fruit of the vine!"[1] He lifted the stone goblet to his lips and sipped the sweet red wine before handing it to John. John took a sip, and then the cup was passed to Judas and around the rest of the table.

Jesus looked around the table at His disciples as they passed the cup. He had only hours left with them. He looked into their eyes and deep into their hearts and found there still remained dangerous flaws of pride and selfish ambition. Even on this, the night of the Paschal feast, when all was to be joy and thanksgiving, they had been quarrelling about who was the greatest among them.

When the last person to finish had taken the final sip, the time had come in the meal for the ceremonial washing of hands. Jesus rose from His position at the table and walked toward the basin and pitcher of water. But to the astonishment of the disciples, He did not fill it and pass it around the table according to custom. Instead, Jesus pulled His outer garment off over His head and hung it on a nearby hook. Then He reached for a towel and tied it around His waist as a common slave would.

Peter watched the water splash from the pitcher into the basin in the lamplight. Without a word, Jesus knelt behind John and placed the basin beneath his feet.

He dipped his hands into the water to pour it over John's feet,
gently washing away the dirt and grime of Jerusalem.

Once they were clean, he took the towel from his waist and dried them before moving to the next man. The room was silent except for the sound of flowing water and the rise and fall of the basin until Jesus came to Peter.

"Lord, are you going to wash my feet?" he asked incredulously (John 13:6).

Jesus looked at him for a long moment and then gently responded, *"You do not realize now what I am doing, but later you will understand"* (John 13:7).

But Peter, despite his good intentions, was still far from understanding the true nature of the kingdom of God. His heart had yet to be tendered for service by the fires of devastating trial and failure.

"No," Peter shook his head stubbornly. "You shall never wash my feet."

Jesus looked at Peter. He saw all that lay before him and all the promise still unrealized inside him. The stakes were simply too high for Him to discard so important a lesson.

"Unless I wash you, you have no part with me" (John 13:8).

"Then, Lord, not just my feet but my hands and head as well!" (John 13:9).

Jesus poured water over Peter's feet and began to wash away the filth of the streets and the residue of his day's labors.

"Those who have had a bath need only wash their feet; their whole body is clean. And you are clean, though not every one of you." Jesus spoke quietly as He wrapped Peter's feet in the towel and glanced across the table to where dark shadows fell across Judas's face in the flickering lamplight. (John 13:10).

Jesus rose from His position in front of Peter and then walked across the room to return the basin. He untied the towel, laid it aside, and pulled His garment over His head before retaking His seat. Then He took a long look around the table at the men who were His closest friends and to whom the most important work in the history of mankind would soon be entrusted. It was a mission that could be accomplished only through the power of great humility and a leadership defined by servanthood.

"Do you understand what I have done for you?" Jesus asked them. *"You call me 'Teacher' and 'Lord', and rightly so, for that is what I am. Now that I, your Lord and Teacher, have washed your feet, you also should wash one another's feet. I have set you an example that you should do as I have done for you. Very truly I tell you, no servant is greater than his master, nor is a messenger greater than the one who sent him. Now that you know these things, you will be blessed if you do them."* (John 13:12–17)

Then Jesus reached for some of the bitter herbs, dipped them in salt water, and ate some before passing them on to the others. Bitter herbs— symbolic of the bondage in Egypt and, on this poignant night, representative of the bondage of all creation—were partaken of by the Lamb of God who would soon be slain for the redemption of all mankind. Very soon, Jesus Himself would be presented as the perfect sacrifice. Spotless. Undefiled. Not one bone would be broken.

Prayer

Perfect Lamb of God,

What do I, a redeemed child of the fall, know of the kingdom of God? Your thoughts are not my thoughts. Your ways are not my ways.[2]

Change me, O God. Teach me the power of humility and the beauty of servanthood so that I will seek Your kingdom first, foremost, and until the very end.

Amen

1. Edersheim, *The Life and Times of Jesus the Messiah*, pg 496
2. Isaiah 55:8

GETHSEMANE

After he has suffered,
he will see the light of life and be satisfied;
by his knowledge my righteous servant will justify many,
and he will bear their iniquities.
Therefore I will give him a portion among the great,
and he will divide the spoils with the strong,
because he poured out his life unto death,
and was numbered with the transgressors.
For he bore the sin of many,
and made intercession for the transgressors.

ISAIAH 53:11–12

Before you begin, read Luke 22:39–48; Matthew 26:36–46; and John 18:1–11

A BRIGHT SPRING MOON lit the way for the eleven of us that night as we followed Jesus through the streets of Jerusalem. The city was busy despite the late hour. Lamplight flickered from the windows of closely packed homes as the many faithful prepared to go to the temple. The gates would groan open at midnight to receive floods of pilgrims into the magnificent courts for the Feast of Unleavened Bread.

Soon, we left the heart of Jerusalem behind and passed the Pool of Israel* to exit the city gate. A moment later, we crossed the lofty bridge which spanned the Kidron Valley.* I peered over the edge into the darkness below as the sound of rushing water rose to meet me. Once we crossed the bridge, it was only a short walk up the Mount of Olives to Gethsemane, our familiar retreat.

Gethsemane belonged to a follower of Jesus who graciously offered us access anytime we were in the city. Over the months we had lingered there for many pleasant hours behind the quiet walls listening to the Lord's teachings. Occasionally, when the city was crowded with pilgrims during festivals, we even spent the night.

The garden was graced with a variety of flowering shrubs and fruit trees, but the olive trees were both its primary produce and the origin of its name, for *Gethsemane* simply means "oil press." Later, when we looked back on that night, we would realize the poignant significance of the place and the name. For in Gethsemane Jesus was hard pressed for all humanity.

After we entered the garden, we stopped at the building that housed the oil press. The interior was quiet and the large round stone in the center of the olive press was motionless, for the olive harvest was still months away. The trees in the garden had yet to even set fruit beneath their thin, silvery leaves. Jesus turned to the eleven of us.

"Sit here while I go over there and pray" (Matthew 26:36).

He motioned to James, John, and me to follow Him farther into the garden. That was when I first realized something was desperately wrong. What was it that passed through His eyes in the moonlight? Grief? Sorrow? Dread? My heart stilled. Always, He had been so sure, so deliberate with each new step . . . even when the rest of us were paralyzed by fear.

Jesus took a few steps more and stopped. He placed a hand on my arm, and when He spoke, His voice was strained.

"My soul is overwhelmed with sorrow to the point of death. Stay here and keep watch with me" (Matthew 26:38).

We stood in stunned silence as Jesus walked a short distance away. He fell to His knees and bowed low until He lay face down in the dust. We all sat down without ever taking our eyes off of Him as He began reverently praying and weeping. Our Lord, our *Friend,* was suffering. The three of us lay prostrate on the ground and joined Him in prayer. The moments slipped by as His anguished cries shattered the silence of the night. I remember that, when Jesus called out to God for deliverance, Jesus called Him "Father."

"Abba, Father," He said, *"everything is possible for you. Take this cup from me. Yet not what I will, but what you will"* (Mark 14:36).

The next thing I knew, Jesus was shaking me awake.

"Simon," He said, *"are you asleep?"* His face above me was lined with strain, and His voice was urgent. *"Couldn't you keep watch for one hour? Watch and pray so that you will not fall into temptation. The spirit is willing, but the flesh is weak"* (Mark 14:37–38).

I sat up and leaned over to awaken James and John as Jesus returned to pray.

Once again, Jesus lay face down and began crying out to God. The moments slipped by as sobs shook His body, until slowly His weeping subsided. He lay deathly still from exhaustion.

Then an angel appeared to Him and Jesus was renewed. He immediately began praying with new fervency. Again and again He asked for God's deliverance and yet proclaimed His desire to do God's will. Bright moonlight flooded the garden as His face became drenched with sweat. To our horror, the sweat on His brow began to be mixed with blood. It ran down His face, mingled with His tears, and fell in great drops onto the ground.

———————

At the time, all we knew was that something was wrong, very wrong. We didn't understand that Jesus was fighting one of the key battles in the war for our redemption, a redemption He would purchase by walking through the valley of death.

> *How could we comprehend how unspeakably*
> *horrible the anticipation of death was for Him?*

All men fear death, of course. We fear the pain of death and the relinquishment of this life, but it was different for Him. We are the children of the fall, born with the fingerprints of death on our souls, and although we fear it, there is something of it that is forever familiar to us. Not so for Jesus. He was born sinless, and though He submitted Himself to be enrobed in human flesh, death was all together foreign to the Giver of Life. How could He who knew no death bear the thought of drinking every last drop from the cup of death for all humanity? This was His anguish in the garden.[1] How could we fathom such suffering? We were children witnessing the epic battle of a King.

Full of good intentions and all the love our childish hearts could offer, we stretched out our frames onto the dust to pray with Him once again.

But before I knew it, sleep had claimed me, and Jesus was bending over me once again. His voice was still urgent; His eyes still filled with sorrow. This time traces of blood streaked his brow. We didn't even know what to say to Him.

He left us to return to the anguish of His prayers. The torrent of His weeping, His begging for deliverance, and His yielding to the will of the Father seemed to fall endlessly on the shores of heaven.

I looked at James and John and saw my heartbreak for Jesus mirrored in their eyes. We watched Him helplessly for a moment before returning with heavy hearts to our own prayers. A breeze drifted through Gethsemane, carrying with it the scent of roses and the heavy sweetness of fig trees as I begged God to come to Jesus' aid and strengthen us all for whatever lay ahead. James, John, and I prayed and wept with Jesus. But as the night stretched long, the heavy sorrow in our hearts overwhelmed our bodies and our minds as well, and we drifted off to sleep once again.

When Jesus awakened me for the last time, He was different. Streaks of blood-tinged sweat remained on His brow, but His face was calm; His eyes, resolute. He spoke gently, calmly..

"Are you still sleeping and resting? Look, the hour has come, and the Son of Man is delivered into the hands of sinners. Rise! Let us go! Here comes my betrayer!" (Matthew 26:45–46).

We scrambled to our feet to confront this betrayer, but the garden remained silent and serene in the moonlight. James, John, and I looked at each other in bewilderment. Jesus calmly began walking back toward Gethsemane's gate, so we followed Him.

We passed underneath the branches of olive trees fringed with silvery leaves. We had spent so many wonderful hours against their ancient, gnarled trunks, talking together and listening as Jesus taught us about the kingdom of God. It was almost as if our laughter could still be heard drifting through the branches above. Each step we took was rich with memories. We had eaten together, worked together, and seen the glory of God fall from heaven by Christ's hand. We had no way of knowing that, as we drew nearer to the garden gate, we were closer to leaving that cherished season of our lives behind forever. For in those moments, the garden was still. The world as we knew it had yet to be shattered.

We arrived at the entrance a moment before Judas arrived with a huge crowd of men behind him. He looked shocked to find us waiting for him; I suppose he expected to find us asleep. Immediately behind Judas were the representatives of the high priests. To their rear was an armed Roman cohort of around two hundred soldiers. The men were armed with clubs and swords. They also carried torches and lanterns on poles to search the shadowy corners of Gethsemane for Jesus. They would not need their weapons or even their lanterns, for they would find no resistance. None at all.

The crowd amassed behind Judas awaiting his move, but he hesitated, so Jesus took charge.

"*Who is it you want?*" Jesus asked them (John 18:4).

From somewhere in the crowd came the sneering, contemptuous reply. "Jesus the Nazarene" (John 18:7 MSG).

Then Jesus' authoritative, courageous response: "*I am he*" (John 18:5).

Those in the front of the crowd stumbled and fell back onto the ground at Jesus' answer. Perhaps they were stunned by His courage or feared a display of His power. A heavy silence hung in the air as they struggled to their feet.

The high priest's representatives began to glance awkwardly at Judas as if awaiting his move. It was a moment that Caiaphas the high priest had been working toward for a long time.

He had been determined to kill Jesus after
He raised Lazarus from the dead.

It seemed he considered Jesus' popularity with the masses a personal threat. As a result, Caiaphas famously declared that it was better "that one man die for the people than that the whole nation perish" (John 11:50). Ironically, it was Caiaphas' privilege as the high priest to recognize the coming of Messiah. His statement, which he intended for evil and personal gain, was ultimately a fulfillment of his priestly role. As John said, "He did not say this on his own, but as high priest that year he prophesied that Jesus would die for the Jewish nation, and not only for that nation but also for the scattered children of God, to bring them together and make them one" (John 11:51–52).

Judas glanced back at the high priest's officials, took a deep breath, and stepped forward to Jesus.

"Greetings, Rabbi!" Judas said as he began covering Jesus' face with kisses (Matthew 26:49). Jesus stood silently, enduring the indignity. When Judas stepped back, Jesus raised His eyes to meet His betrayer's.

"Do what you came for, friend," He said sadly (Matthew 26:50).

Judas' face fell. He took a halting step backward.

Once again, Jesus turned to the crowd. He squared His shoulders and addressed them.

"Who is it you want?" Jesus asked them again.

"Jesus of Nazareth," they said (John 18:7).

Jesus turned to motion to us, His eyes filled with love.

"I told you that I am he. If you are looking for me, then let these men go" (John 18:8).

By this time, from inside the olive press, all the other disciples had heard the commotion and gathered behind us. Earlier that very night, Jesus had prayed over us, proclaiming to God that He had kept all of us safe. That prayer was especially significant to me, considering what I did next and what the consequences could have been.

I realized that the men were about to seize Jesus. These were representatives of our priests! Such corruption and injustice! Unfortunately, corruption in the priesthood was not new to us. Every Jewish boy grew up hearing the story of the Hasmonaean ruler Matthais Antigonus.* Even when Matthais was captured, bound, and taken before Herod the Great's puppet high priest, John Hyrcanus,* he found a way to proclaim that the priesthood had become corrupt. Matthias knew that no man could serve in the priesthood if he had a deformity of any kind, so when John Hyrcanus came near to him, Matthias leaned forward and bit off his ear! Corrupt Hyrcanus was thereby disqualified from serving as high priest ever again.

I also had a statement to make about a corrupt priesthood, but unlike Matthias, I still had an actual weapon. All of us who were from Galilee carried short swords hidden in our upper garments, and as a skilled fisherman, I was very good with a knife. So I slipped my weapon from the folds of my robe and, with a deft flick of my wrist, Malchus, the servant of the high priest, lost his ear that night. Malchus screamed in pain and, clutching the side of his head, fell to the ground. It was most certainly enough to grant me a terrible punishment, but Jesus intervened.

*He knelt to the ground and picked up the ear.
Gently, He pulled Malchus's hand away from
his head and simply . . . reattached the ear.*

Malchus gingerly reached up to feel his ear and began to laugh with relief. A stunned silence fell over the crowd as Jesus turned to me.

"Put your sword away! Shall I not drink the cup the Father has given me?" (John 18:11).

Once again, Jesus turned to the crowd as if He were prompting them to finish the task at hand.

"Am I leading a rebellion," said Jesus, *"that you have come out with swords and clubs to capture me? Every day I was with you, teaching in the temple courts, and you did not arrest me. But the Scriptures must be fulfilled"* (Mark 14:48–49).

At this, they seized and bound Him, He who was so obviously giving Himself up willingly.

And us? We ran. We took flight to escape the swords and the clubs. We fled the torchlight to hide in the shadows. As I ran, I cast one last look over my shoulder to see Jesus alone in a crowd of His enemies, swept away into the night. How could I fail to remember in that moment that He had predicted our abandonment of Him only hours before when we had safely sat around the Paschal table?

"A time is coming and in fact has come when you will be scattered, each to your own home. You will leave me all alone" (John 16:32).

We had protested, proclaiming our devotion, but Jesus knew better. Even then, He was thinking of us. He wanted us to know that no matter how dire our circumstances seem, God remains forever faithful.

"Yet I am not alone," Jesus had continued, *"for my Father is with me. I have told you these things, so that in me you may have peace. In this world you will have trouble. But take heart! I have overcome the world"* (John 16:32–33).

Jesus knew then what we would not understand until much later— though He would suffer, it would be no accident. It was part of a divine plan, one He would embrace with courage and majesty. The cup of death, even drunk to its bitter dregs, was not the end.

Death would reign for a moment, but when Jesus arose again, it would be with life for all of us. His victory was a war won on the cross and in the tomb.

But it was a war first fought under the moon, in the still of Gethsemane.

Prayer

My Suffering Savior,

Thank You for wrestling for my redemption in the dark agony of Gethsemane. You, who had never tasted of death, drank the bitter cup of it to its dregs for all humanity. Though perfect and sinless, You bore the sins of many so that You would make intercession for a child of the fall like me.

How can I thank You? Words are a frail offering. My noblest deeds are like a child's trinkets compared to Your infinite worth.

Take my life, King Jesus. Though broken and battered by sin, my life is all I have to give. Gratefully, I place it in Your gentle hands.

I love You.

Amen

1. Based on *The Life and Times of Jesus the Messiah*, Alfred Edersheim.

PETER'S DENIAL

"I have seen their ways, but I will heal them;
*   I will guide them and restore comfort to Israel's mourners,*
*   creating praise on their lips.*
Peace, peace, to those far and near,"
*   says the LORD. "And I will heal them."*

ISAIAH 57:18–19

"SIMON, SIMON, SATAN HAS *asked to sift all of you as wheat. But I have prayed for you, Simon, that your faith may not fail. And when you have turned back, strengthen your brothers*" (Luke 22:31–32).

Peter declared, "Even if all fall away, I will not" (Mark 14:29). "Lord, I am ready to go with you to prison and to death" (Luke22:33).

"I tell you, Peter, before the rooster crows today, you will deny three times that you know me" (Luke 22:34).

Peter was determined to prove Jesus wrong. When the silence of the garden had been shattered by betrayal and sword, Peter had drawn his weapon. When the others fled into the night, Peter joined John in following their Lord and Friend to learn of His fate.

Now, the torchlight bobbed along ahead of them as they struggled to quiet their breath and cling to the shadows. Their eyes never left the mass of heavily armed Roman guards as it coursed through the street before them. Dogs barked as frightened residents peered anxiously out of their windows at the sound of marching sandals and clinking armor. Though they could not see Him, Peter and John knew Jesus was somewhere in the center of the mob of angry men.

Bit by bit, the terrain before them steepened as they left behind the more modest dwellings of the middle class and entered the eastern slope of the Upper City, the home of the aristocracy, awash in luxury and wealth. It was a world of sprawling mansions, servants, priceless furnishings, and breathtaking views. These were the homes of the high priests.

The guards in front slowed their pace and stopped at the largest residence on the block, the home of the high priest Annas.

Peter looked at John and saw relief wash over his face in the moonlight. John reached up and placed a hand on Peter's shoulder.

"Come," he said. "I know Annas. I have been here many times. We can go inside."

John led the way, falling in line behind the group proceeding through the entrance in front of them. A servant girl stood at the doorway, scanning the faces of each person entering the residence. When she saw John, a brief look of recognition flickered through her eyes, and she said nothing. When Peter tried to follow, she stopped him.

"No, I'm sorry."

"But I'm with him," Peter protested, motioning to the rapidly disappearing back of John.

The servant girl just shook her head and began to close the gate.

Peter began pacing back and forth in front of the house. He paused, took one last look at the unflinching face of the servant girl staring back at him through the gate and then looked up at the impenetrable two-story structure looming before him. He walked over to the wall and leaned wearily against it.

He had promised Jesus he would be faithful no matter what, and now he couldn't even get in the door.

For a moment all was still, and then Peter began to hear hushed voices, the turning of the key in the lock, and the creaking of the gate as it swung open. He turned just in time to see John step outside and motion for him to follow. The girl gazed at him suspiciously as he passed, and as he and John descended the steps into the residence, he felt her eyes follow him.

At the bottom of the steps, Peter entered the vestibule. A beautiful mosaic graced the center of the floor. Elaborate patterns swirled in red, blue, and yellow around a large rosette in the center. Pomegranates, symbolic of the priesthood, were inlaid into the corners of the design. A small table rested against the left wall of the vestibule between two doors. Both led into the expansive reception hall where the proceedings were taking place.

John motioned to Peter to go into the courtyard at the end of the hall to wait before slipping inside to be with Jesus. Peering inside the room for a moment, Peter saw that it could easily accommodate a large group. The stucco that covered walls had been treated to give the appearance of stone panels. The ceiling was equally elaborate: there the stucco was imprinted with a complex, intertwining geometric design. Lamplight flickered against the opulence of the space, the magnificent architecture, the luxurious furnishings, and, at last, the crowd of people who seethed with fury. Jesus, still bound, was standing silently in the center.

Tearing his eyes away from the scene, Peter turned to gain his bearings. To the right of the vestibule was another room, even more lavishly decorated than the reception hall. The walls were completely covered with frescoes in rich reds and bold yellows depicting various architectural elements. Peter turned and made his way to the end of the vestibule to enter the courtyard.

Various rooms flanked the large, flagstone-paved courtyard that anchored the home. Another spacious wing, equal in size to the one Peter had just exited, stretched along the far end. This night, the courtyard was a busy place. The guards had gathered there to await further instructions from the officials inside the home. Because the night was cold, someone had already begun a fire in a brazier in the center of the yard. Peter cautiously made his way to the edge of the group and found a seat.

Lamplight from the tall windows of the reception hall fell into the courtyard below, and though Peter could not be inside to witness the proceedings, he could hear the high priests questioning Jesus.

"I have spoken openly to the world," Jesus replied. "I always taught in synagogues or at the temple, where all the Jews come together. I said nothing in secret. Why question me? Ask those who heard me. Surely they know what I said" (John 18:20–21).

Peter winced as the sound of the high priest's palm striking Jesus' face drifted across the courtyard and then gave way to the angry rumblings of the crowd.

At that moment, a servant girl crossed the courtyard from the east wing of the house, carrying a large, ornate, green glass pitcher. She slowed when she saw Peter and then paused to look at him closely.

"You were also with that Nazarene, Jesus," she said.

The guards turned to look at him suspiciously. Peter quickly stood to his feet and angrily responded, "I don't know or understand what you're talking about," he said (Mark 14:67–68).

Peter moved closer to the entrance and away from the crowd.

Meanwhile, the voices from inside the hall were growing louder and angrier by the moment. Peter heard the voice of the high priest rise above the din: "I charge you under oath by the living God: Tell us if you are the Messiah, the Son of God" (Matthew 26:63).

A moment of heavy silence followed, then came Jesus' voice, calm and strong.

"*You have said so,*" Jesus replied. "*But I say to all of you: From now on you will see the Son of Man sitting at the right hand of the Mighty One and coming on the clouds of heaven*" (Matthew 26:64).

"Blasphemy!" the high priest cried as he reached up and grasped the collar of his robe with both hands and tore the robe in two.

"What do you think?" he demanded of the crowd. "What should we do with this man?"

The hall erupted as screams demanding Jesus' death mixed with the sounds of His being beaten at the hands of the court.

Peter was shaking as he made his way back to the fire. As he sat down, one of the men there nodded his head and pointed in his direction. "Surely you are one of them; your accent gives you away" (Matthew 26:73).

Once again, Peter leaped to his feet. "I don't know the man!" he shouted (Matthew 26:74).

One of the high priest's servants took a step closer to him. "Didn't I see you with him in the garden?" (John 18:26).

Again, Peter vehemently denied any personal knowledge of Jesus. At that moment, the first rays of sunrise drifted over the wall and fell in shining beams of gold at Peter's feet. Nearby, at the temple, a priest lifted a large *shofar* to his lips and blew three long blasts—the "cock crow"* that announced the beginning of the liturgical day.

Peter gasped at the sound. He shrank back from the glow of the fire to disappear into the receding shadows and move toward the door. As he passed through the vestibule, he glanced into the reception hall. Jesus, bruised and bleeding, turned to look at him with great sorrow in His eyes. Peter shook his head in horror at his own betrayal. Tears blurred his vision and ran down his cheeks into his beard.

He ran across the vestibule, up the stairs, through the gate, and into the early morning light. He had been so sure of his love, his commitment, his resolve—yet, overcome by fear, he had failed to stand by Jesus. All that was left was to cling to another hope entirely, a strength beyond himself, a promise that though he had fallen he would rise from the ashes once again.

"I have prayed for you, Simon, that your faith may not fail. And when you have turned back, strengthen your brothers" (Luke 22:32).

Prayer

My Redeemer,

I find the most difficult person I have to forgive is me, especially when I am surprised by the fragility of my character and the weakness of my resolve. You said once that the poor in spirit would be blessed. I think, perhaps, I am poorer in spirit than I know.

Your unfathomable grace is the true source of my strength. Help me to cling to the sure promise of Your forgiveness when I fall. Then, from the ashes, I will rise again.

Amen

NOT OF THIS WORLD

—

Jesus Before Pilate

"I will pour out on the house of David and the inhabitants of Jerusalem a spirit of grace and supplication. They will look on me, the one they have pierced, and they will mourn for him as one mourns for an only child, and grieve bitterly for him as one grieves for a firstborn son."

ZECHARIAH 12:10

Before you begin, read John 18:28—19:16 and Matthew 27:11—26

Pontius Pilate was flanked by his personal guards as he strode purposefully into the courtyard. Early morning light was just beginning to stream into the lush gardens of the opulent former residence of Herod the Great. Now, the palace provided a luxurious refuge for Pilate whenever circumstances demanded he leave his more permanent residence of Caesarea Maritima, which overlooked the beautiful Mediterranean Sea. It was especially important that his presence be felt in Jerusalem during the times of the feasts to keep the populace in check. His time as procurator over Judea had been . . . tumultuous. He simply couldn't afford another riot. Rome was watching.

Pilate sat down in an ornately carved chair that he had earlier ordered to be placed at the top of the short flight of steps leading to the courtyard. A small group of men, Jewish leaders, stood directly in front of him. The men, many of them from the Jewish priesthood, had refused to enter his home for the meeting because they considered Gentile homes unclean.

Another Man stood quietly in the center of the crowd with His hands bound. The gathering had to wait only a moment for Pilate, but He had been ready for them.

"What charges are you bringing against this man?" Pilate demanded (John 18:29).

Pilate watched with satisfaction as his first blow hit home. He knew about the situation, of course. They had approached him the night before to obtain permission to use his soldiers for the arrest. As Pilate watched their flustered faces, his suspicions concerning their expectations of him were confirmed. They thought they could march into his courtyard with their prisoner, trial complete, sentence in place, and manipulate him to do their bidding. His insistence that they bring the charges formally had both surprised and unnerved them. He wasn't exactly sure why they were bringing one of their own to him, but the entire situation had the scent of opportunity to it. If they wanted something from him, he would gain something in return. And he would begin by showing them who was in charge.

One of the men spoke up defensively: "If he were not a criminal, we would not have handed him over to you" (John 18:30).

Pilate stared stonily back at him. When he spoke, his voice was low and dangerous.

"Take Him yourselves and judge him by your own law."

"But we have no right to execute anyone!" they protested.

They couldn't of course. They were impotent—a fact he very much wanted them to remember.

Pilate turned to his guards and motioned to them to bring the prisoner into the palace to be questioned separately.

Then he sat down in the cool of the hall. Graceful columns rose from the intricate mosaic floor to support lofty arches high above him. A green glass platter, laden with honeyed figs and plump grapes, rested on the carved stone table near his right hand. Servants stood throughout the room, as silent and still as statues, awaiting his command. Pilate heard the approach of footsteps. He sat tall in his chair and adjusted the folds of his robe.

The soldiers entered the room and led Jesus to stand before him. Silence blanketed the room as Pilate evaluated Him. Jesus wore a simple unadorned garment, the raiment of the common man. His eyes were bloodshot, and his face creased with exhaustion. Pilate realized the Jewish leaders must have gotten a bit carried away in their interrogations of Him because one cheekbone bore a red mark and had begun to swell. He did not seem to offer any struggle, yet He was bound.

This is it? This is the threat? The usurper-king?

Pilate laughed softly.

"Are You the king of the Jews?" he asked Jesus incredulously. Jesus met Pilate's eyes unflinchingly. He refused to be drawn into his political maneuverings or petty insults. Instead, he appealed straight to the Roman leader's conscience.

"Is that your own idea," Jesus asked, *"or did others talk to you about me?"* (John 18:33–34).

But Pilate's conscience was buried far beneath the stratum of his world-view. He could not conceive of a king enrobed in humility and sacrifice any more than he could accept the Jews as anything other than a despised people.

"Am I a Jew?" Pilate asked. The implication was clear: he couldn't possibly care about such things.

Pilate narrowed his eyes and stared at the prisoner. There was something strange going on. Normally, the Jews would do anything they could to cause trouble for him. Why were the leaders now bringing him one of their own?

"Your own people and the chief priests handed You over to me. What is it You have done?" Pilate asked.

Pilate considered Jesus thoughtfully as he contemplated how the Man before him could have gained such powerful enemies.

Jesus looked at Pilate silently for a moment. The hour of His life was late. He did not have time for meaningless squabbles. Instead of answering the question, Jesus addressed the issue at the heart of the conflict.

"My kingdom is not of this world. If it were, my servants would fight to prevent my arrest by the Jewish leaders. But now my kingdom is from another place" (John 18:36).

"So you are a king then!" Pilate scoffed.

"You say that I am a king. In fact, the reason I was born and came into the world is to testify to the truth. Everyone on the side of truth listens to me" (John 18:37).

The Roman procurator's face darkened. Great philosophers loved to talk about universal truth, but as far as he had seen, there was no truth, not even in the most basic moments of life. It was unobtainable, like trying to grasp the motes of dust in the beams of sunlight that were now flooding through the windows of the hall.

"What is truth?" he asked cynically. Then with a brush of his hand, Pilate dismissed Jesus from the room.

Pilate then rose to gaze out the window at the courtyard below him. A crowd had gathered behind the chief priests and their entourage. The people were assembling in anticipation of the traditional release of a prisoner in honor of Passover. Pilate knew Jesus was wildly popular among the commoners. He was certain some of those gathered had done so in hope of securing His release.

Pilate glanced at a table beside the window and reached down to run his finger along a thin vein in the marble top, a hairline imperfection of potentially dangerous frailty. The people, too, had a dangerous flaw. They were divided, and Pilate fully intended to exploit it to his advantage. He would apply pressure to their vein of division, playing the desires of one against the other while lording his power over them all until he had the concessions he wanted. They would crumble like shattered marble around his feet.

The chief priests had inadvertently surrendered a valuable pawn to him in their bloodlust to take the life of the Galilean prophet. He glanced back out the window with a satisfied smile and then walked briskly out of the room.

A moment later Pilate stepped into the bright morning sunlight. The crowd stilled at his approach.

The Jewish leaders stepped forward importantly, expectantly, but Pilate ignored them and addressed the crowd behind them.

"I find no basis for a charge against him. But it is your custom for me to release to you one prisoner at the time of the Passover. Do you want me to release 'the king of the Jews'?" (John 18:38–39).

Immediately, the ego-bruised chief priests erupted in fury.

"No, not him! Give us Barabbas!" (John 18:40).

Angry shouts mixed with cries for mercy in the courtyard for several moments as Pilate patiently allowed the cauldron of dissension to simmer. He raised his hand to silence the crowd and deliberately turned up the heat.

"What shall I do, then, with Jesus who is called the Messiah?" Pilate asked (Matthew 27:22).

The Jewish leaders had approached Pilate that morning with what seemed to be a perfect plan.

Now, a humiliating defeat was looking both inevitable and imminent. So they held nothing back.

"Crucify him!" (Matthew 27:22).

Shouts of protest erupted from Jesus' supporters as Pilate turned his back on them to enter the palace once again. As he walked, he motioned for a guard to come to him.

"Yes, Procurator."

"Scourge the prisoner and bring Him back to me," Pilate ordered.

Pilate retreated into the cool of the mansion to wait.

A short while later the guard returned.

"The prisoner is ready, Procurator."

"Excellent," Pilate replied. "I will go out to speak to the people first. Bring Him forth on my signal."

Once again, a tense silence fell over the crowd at Pilate's approach.

"Look, I am bringing him out to you to let you know that I find no basis for a charge against him," Pilate said (John 19:4).

He held his hand aloft, signaling to the guards to bring Jesus to stand in front of the crowd. "Here is the man!" he announced dramatically.

Pilate turned to see the guards leading Jesus to the front of the platform. Trembling uncontrollably from pain and shock, He stumbled repeatedly as He struggled to walk. Pilate noted with satisfaction that his men had exceeded his expectations of them. All men emerged from the scourging post bloody, their flesh shredded and torn, but this prisoner had endured special humiliation. They had crowned Him with thorns and placed a purple robe, fit for a king, on His lacerated back. The long thorns had pierced His scalp. Blood matted His hair and coursed down His face.

> *The gasps and wails of horror of Jesus' followers were drowned out by the screams of the men in power.*

These men who had been entrusted with the spiritual leadership of a nation and honored with the task of recognizing and proclaiming Messiah's coming now screamed for His torturous death. The kingdom of God had risen, but they were blinded to its coming.

"Crucify! Crucify!" they chanted.

Pilate pressed harder on the fault of their division, the fatal flaw of their misplaced desires.

"You take him and crucify him. As for me, I find no basis for a charge against him," Pilate answered condescendingly (John 19:6).

The Jewish leaders scrambled for a foothold as their powerlessness was flaunted before them once again.

"We have a law," they protested, "and according to that law he must die, because he claimed to be the Son of God" (John 19:7).

Pilate squinted into the glare of the Middle Eastern sun and then turned to look at the prisoner to his left.

The Son of God?

He motioned for the guards to follow with Jesus as he turned to walk back into the palace.

He sat down in the hall and called for Jesus to be brought before him. Despite the heat, the Man shivered and shook as steady drops of blood fell onto the mosaic floor beneath His feet.

"Where do you come from?" Pilate asked Him (John 19:9).

But Jesus stared at the floor and said nothing.

Pilate was enraged. He leaned forward in his seat and shouted.

"Do you refuse to speak to me?" Pilate said. "Don't you realize I have power either to free or to crucify you?" (John 19:10).

Slowly, Jesus lifted His head to look at him. One eye was almost swollen shut, and His face was bloody and bruised. He looked steadily into Pilate's furious face for a long moment before speaking.

"You would have no power over me if it were not given to you from above. Therefore the one who handed me over to you is guilty of a greater sin" (John 19:11).

The implication was clear. Power was a divine trust, and Pilate had violated that trust over and again through his abuse of his position. But similarly the Jewish leaders had been entrusted with power in both the judicial realm and the spiritual. They had corrupted both to build and defend a kingdom of their own design.

Pilate dismissed Jesus once again, and servants moved immediately to clean the floor where He had stood. The procurator rose to absentmindedly watch the crowd from his window again. Earlier, his wife had admonished him to have nothing to do with the Man because of the dreams she had the previous night. He had always been taught that dreams were messages from the gods. Didn't this Man say His kingdom was not of this world? Surely, he had not scourged the son of a god . . .

But no, it didn't make any sense. What god would allow himself to be scourged? What god would submit willingly to the bonds of mere men? This man could not possibly be king or god.

Pilate shook himself free of the anxious thoughts and returned his attention to the crowd below. He could still win. He knew it.

He walked back outside and quieted the crowd.

"I have decided to set him free."

The Jewish leaders shouted back the best threat they could devise.

"If you let this man go, you are no friend of Caesar. Anyone who claims to be a king opposes Caesar" (John 19:12).

Pilate was not afraid. They were moving ever closer to his trap. Immediately, he called for Jesus to be brought to Gabbatha, the Stone Pavement.* He was almost ready to pronounce judgment. He sat down and then turned to the Jewish leaders.

"Here is your king," he said scornfully.

But they shouted, *"Take him away! Take him away! Crucify him!"* (John 19:14–15).

They were almost there. Just another push . . .

"Shall I crucify your king?" Pilate asked.

"We have no king but Caesar," the chief priests answered.

Victory. Pilate sat back in his chair and smiled. They had sworn the allegiance they had been determined never to give. His instincts had been right. The Galilean prophet had been a very valuable pawn after all. There would be no more riots and no more dreaded councils sent to Rome to report on all he had been doing out of the Emperor's sight. His rule was secure.

He wasn't quite finished ridiculing them yet, though.

He stood and called for a golden bowl of water to be brought. Ceremoniously, and with great pomp, he washed his hands, mocking the Jewish rite for the atonement of an unsolved murder as outlined in the book of Deuteronomy.[1]

"I am innocent of this man's blood," Pilate said. "It is your responsibility" (Matthew 27:24).

The message was sent and received. He wanted them to know he saw through their pious guise to their corrupt hearts, lustful for power.

The chief priests' steely reply returned without pause as Jesus' supporters began to weep.

"His blood is on us and our children!" (Matthew 27:25).

Pilate laughed softly, shook the water from his hands, and then motioned toward Jesus without looking at Him.

"Take him and crucify him."[2]

The Jewish leaders turned to go to their service at the temple. They had negotiated away their loyalty to the One True King in order to preserve their own position. Pilate returned to his palace to savor the thrill of a winning a vital political battle. He gazed up at Herod the Great's lofty towers, the Phasael, Mariamme, and Hippicus.* He was confident he would be enjoying Herod's many beautiful homes for a long time.

Jesus turned to carry His crossbeam to Golgotha. He was just collateral damage in the eyes of Pilate and the Jewish leaders, a pawn to be played. In truth, His journey to the cross was the fulfillment of His kingly duty; it was a victory won. Each suffering step through Jerusalem's streets was graced with divine majesty. Every drop of sweat and blood was like a royal jewel strewn in the dust. It was a procession so majestic that the very angels of heaven paused in holy stillness to watch it.

His kingdom is not of this world.

Prayer

My King,

The temporal draws my flesh like the moon calls the tide. I am wooed by promises of power, and I am enamored with shining baubles that turn to ashes in my hands.

Yet I want to be a loyal citizen of heaven. So give me a relentless vision for eternity and an unremitting delight for a kingdom that never fades.

Amen

1. Deuteronomy 21:1–9
2. This is not expressly stated in the text but implied in the John account.

NEVER TOO FAR

The Thief on the Cross

He was despised and rejected by mankind,
   a man of suffering, and familiar with pain.
Like one from whom people hide their faces
   he was despised, and we held him in low esteem.
Surely he took up our pain
   and bore our suffering,
yet we considered him punished by God,
   stricken by him, and afflicted.
But he was pierced for our transgressions,
   he was crushed for our iniquities;
the punishment that brought us peace was on him,
   and by his wounds we are healed.

ISAIAH 53:3–5

"WHAT A WASTE OF a good nail."

These were the first words he heard as he regained consciousness. The two Roman guards sat on their haunches to inspect the seven-inch piece of iron they had just struggled to drive through his right heel. The nail was most certainly now too bent to be reused. It had passed through the block on the outside of his ankle, placed there to ensure it would not pull loose from his body, then expertly torn through his flesh. But it had stubbornly refused to become fully embedded into the olive tree from which he now hung.

His body shook violently with tremors from the pain and the muscle spasms that were already setting in from hanging in such an awkward position. The nails in his arms and ankles sent searing pain along his nerve paths. The rough wood of the tree dug into the lacerations on his back left by the de-fleshing of the flagellum. The sedile,* a wooden block seat, was especially efficient. It dug into his buttocks, both prolonging his life and increasing his agony. None of it compared to the torture of inhaling for breath, any breath, and the pain that accompanied the slightest effort.

At that moment, he could endure suffocation no longer and pushed against the nails in his ankles to lift himself high enough to draw another breath. He cried out in agony, and his body trembled more violently.

"Must have been a knot in the wood," the second soldier said as he slapped his friend on the shoulder in consolation for a job less than perfectly done. The two men rose to their feet to turn their attention to the third and last condemned man of the day.

A stream of curses drew Jehohanan's attention. He turned his gaze to his right to see Simeon a short distance away on his own cross. Simeon was filled with rage even now when his fury was most certainly spent in vain.

Jehohanan gasped for air and returned his attention to the brutal drama unfolding beneath him.

On the ground, the third Man still knelt slumped next to His cross-beam awaiting His turn with the hammer and nail. He already looked more dead than alive. His face was bruised and swollen. Someone had pulled out large patches of His beard exposing raw skin underneath. He had lost huge amounts of blood from the crown of inch-long thorns the soldiers had driven into His scalp when they mocked Him as Israel's king. It all had a terrible irony to it. This was the man half of Judea thought was the "Messiah come at last" to set them free from Roman oppression. The guards had even put the title "Jesus of Nazareth, King of the Jews" on the name plaque on His cross. Now, He was suffering the humiliation and torment of Roman crucifixion.

Some king, Jehohanan thought. *He didn't even fight when they led Him to the posts for the scourging. He simply offered His back to them as meekly as a lamb. How dare He? How dare He just give up when He had the will of the people behind Him? No stirring speech. No valiant ending. Just surrender.*

Jehohanan struggled upward for another breath and blinding pain washed over him. Then, somewhere from long ago, a passage his rabbi taught him as a boy drifted back to him. It was one of the Servant Songs of Isaiah.*

> *I offered my back to those who beat me,*
> *my cheeks to those who pulled out my beard.*
> Isaiah 50:6

If his education at the feet of his rabbi taught him the law of Moses and Servant Songs, it was at the campfire and dinner table where he learned his politics. He remembered the men sitting around the fire passionately discussing the census, Caesar's brazen move to drag into slavery a people set apart to serve God alone.

Zealots rose among the people who were passionate for Israel's freedom at any cost. As far as these men were concerned, there could be no compliance if Israel were to be free. If a neighbor wasn't working with the Zealots, he was a conspirator with the enemy. If he lost his property or his life, so be it. There were moments when the line between patriotism and oppression was dangerously blurred. In those dark hours there were those among them who became malefactors, murderers, criminals, thieves.

Jehohanan glanced down at this One who meekly gave His body to the oppressor and remembered all the dark nights when he had returned home to his wife and child, his hands and blade stained with blood in his pursuit of his own life of crime. He would scrub his hands clean, but his heart would remain heavy with guilt as he sat before the dying firelight while his family slept. But the impulse to steal was strong; and no matter how many times he vowed to become an honest man, he returned to his thievery over and again.

The crowd of observers gasped as the soldiers stripped the third Man and moved to force Him to the crossbeam, but they found no resistance to their touch. He did not fight, scream for mercy, curse, or try to run. When the moment came for the first nail, it almost seemed as if the Man put His wrist in place to receive it.

Jehohanan tried to shift on the sedile to find a way to alleviate his suffering, but to no avail, while beside him the torturous process of raising the third Man's cross began. Slowly, excruciatingly, the crossbeam rose until, at last, it was secured. Many men curse as nails, flesh, and gravity meet.

Most men cry out and beg for mercy, but not this Man.
Though clearly in horrific pain, He didn't utter a word.

Jehohanan lifted himself up for another gasp of breath, and then the torment of suffocation began once again. Tears began coursing down his cheeks as the rough wood of the cross raked across his raw back.

Somewhere through the haze of pain, more of Isaiah's Servant Song drifted back through his mind as he considered the silent Man beside him.

> He was oppressed and afflicted,
>   yet he did not open his mouth;
> he was led like a lamb to the slaughter,
>   and as a sheep before its shearers is silent,
> so he did not open his mouth.
>
> Isaiah 53:7

Two crosses over, Simeon was cursing again, but now his attention was drawn away from the guards to the Man on the center cross as he heaped curses on Him in His suffering. Jesus' eyes, however, were on the guards at His feet who were casting lots for the garment they had just stripped from Him. At last, He broke His silence.

"Father, forgive them, for they do not know what they are doing" (Luke 23:34).

Jehohanan needed another breath. He gritted his teeth, pushed against the nails in his ankles, and sent jolts of pain up his legs. He cried out in agony as he sank down again. Jesus turned to the sound of his cry, and His eyes were filled with a compassion that disarmed Jehohanan. Unbelievably, this Man who suffered in silence was offering him what kindness He could give, *from His own cross.*

Hours of blinding pain drifted by as muscle spasms shook Jehohanan's body. His lungs ached for air, and his mouth grew dry. Beside him the Man spoke again, this time to a friend on the ground. He asked the friend to care for His mother after His death. As Jehohanan struggled against the nails for breath, he glanced at the Man in the middle again and then at the soldiers below. The Man's composure in the midst of such unspeakable suffering seemed to strip the soldiers of their power to invoke terror in the crowd. Jehohanan couldn't shake the thought that the soldiers were simply playing a part in something that was infinitely larger than they realized. In fact, the soldiers were not taking this Man's life; He was giving it.

Did not the Servant Song reflect this Man who did "not shout or cry out, or raise his voice in the streets" (Isaiah 42:2)? What if the Messiah was not in fact meant to establish His rule over sand and stone but in the kingdom of God Himself far above the heavens?

And if that were the case, Jehohanan thought as a sob escaped his cracked and swollen lips, then all was not lost.

His lungs burned for air again, and once again he pushed against the nails as wave after wave of excruciating pain washed over him. He gasped for breath and then sank back down against the torturous sedile, the cruel nails. Jehohanan dropped his chin to his chest. He blinked salty tears out of his eyes, and his naked body, bruised and bleeding, came into focus. The shame was more than he could bear.

Through his torment, the voice of his rabbi reciting the Servant Songs came back to him once again.

> *Who among you fears the* LORD
> *and obeys the word of his servant?*
> *Let the one who walks in the dark,*
> *who has no light,*
> *trust in the name of the* LORD
> *and rely on their God.*
>
> ISAIAH 50:10

His thoughts were broken by a fresh resurgence of Simeon's curses directed toward the Man on the center cross. Simeon. Violent in life. Violent in death. Violent to the bitter end.

Jehohanan struggled to catch another precious breath and then turned to Simeon.

"Don't you fear God," he said, "since you are under the same sentence? We are punished justly, for we are getting what our deeds deserve. But this man has done nothing wrong" (Luke 23:40–41).

Jehohanan looked at Jesus. His voice broke, and fresh tears ran down his face. Tears of brokenness. Tears of repentance. And, against all odds, tears of hope.

"Jesus, remember me when you come into your kingdom" (Luke 23:42).

It was a hope well placed. Jesus' answer was immediate and full of promise—rescuing the one willing to be found to the very end. Never too late; never too far.

Jesus answered him, *"Truly I tell you, today you will be with me in paradise"* (Luke 23:43).

Prayer

Lamb of God,

By Your power a cruel method of torture and execution was utterly transformed. What all believed to be a curse, You used as a means to be a blessing. What all believed to be a death sentence, You turned into life eternal. In Your hands certain defeat became ultimate victory. From horrific death You brought life to us all.

Thank You that I can never wander so far into sin that I can't come home again. My hope endures as long as I am willing to be found. It is never, ever too late.

Amen

NICODEMUS

I will give them an undivided heart and put a new spirit in them; I will remove from them their heart of stone and give them a heart of flesh. Then they will follow my decrees and be careful to keep my laws. They will be my people, and I will be their God.

EZEKIEL 11:19–20

NICODEMUS DROPPED THE BAG of myrrh and aloes heavily to the ground. The sweet, woodsy scent of the burial spices drifted upward and mixed with the prevalent, metallic scent of blood. Slowly, he raised his eyes to look at the body hanging at eye level on the cross in front of him. The Man in front of him was once so full of life that all He touched was transformed.

Now He was perfectly still, lifeless, and pale.
His hair was matted with dried blood that clung
to the sides of His bruised and swollen face.

Nicodemus took a deep breath and dropped his head with a sigh.

Joseph placed a hand on his shoulder as he blinked away his own tears. Nicodemus stared at the bag at his feet. Costly? Yes, but what did it matter? It was a mere token of devotion given much too late. He heard Joseph clear his throat and then turn to approach the Roman guards and give them the order from Pilate. They were to take down the body and turn it over to these two teachers of Israel, members of the Sanhedrin who had secretly put their faith in Messiah Jesus. How ironic that the curse of the cross would give Joseph and Nicodemus the courage to step into the light once the Teacher was gone.

Nicodemus turned his eyes back to the cross and watched the Roman guards as they hooked a hammer beneath the rim of the seven-inch nail that tethered Jesus' heel to the wood and began to pry it loose. Wincing, Nicodemus closed his eyes and turned his thoughts back in time to that first night when he met Jesus on the rooftop.

He had waited until darkness fell. It was far too risky to be seen. After all, only days before Jesus had made mortal enemies of the Jewish aristocracy when He entered the temple courts and cleared them of those who were buying and selling there. It was extraordinarily dangerous to be found in the company of such a Man, but Nicodemus had seen something in Him that spoke of the truth, and he was willing to risk everything to find out more. So as a spring wind gusted along between the homes and shops of Jerusalem, one of the teachers of Israel, trained in the best schools money could buy, had stepped into the deserted streets to inquire of the young Rabbi from Nazareth. It was a radical deviation from all that was expected and proper, but Nicodemus had been observing Jesus and listening to His teaching. He had lived long enough to recognize remarkable truth when he witnessed it. He wasn't yet ready to risk his position and wealth to pledge his allegiance, but he needed to know more.

Nicodemus carried no lamp and stayed close to the shadows, depending on the moon to light his way. His footsteps on the stone-paved streets were drowned out by the wind. Up and down the narrow streets he climbed, leaving his wealthy neighborhood behind and entering the more humble dwellings of the middle class. Soon he was in front of the home where Jesus was staying. Lamplight still flickered from the windows of the guest room on the roof. He took a deep breath and began to climb the outer staircase to the top.

Nicodemus turned his eyes back to the cross as the first nail pulled free and clinked to the ground. The guard stood, dusted off his hands . . . and then moved to the other side to begin working on the second nail.

Jesus' disciple who had answered the door that night certainly seemed surprised to find a member of the temple leadership on his doorstep, but Jesus had not seemed shocked at all. He had received Nicodemus calmly and confidently. Nicodemus remembered exactly what he had said to Jesus, and it was what he still believed as he stood on windy Golgotha with burial spices and broken hope at his feet.

"We know that you are a teacher who has come from God. For no one could perform the signs you are doing if God were not with him" (John 3:2).

But Jesus had looked right past his words to the deepest cry of his heart.

"*Very truly I tell you, no one can see the kingdom of God unless they are born again*" (John 3:3).

At the time, those words pierced Nicodemus' soul. *How can that be?* he had wondered. He knew all too well that the whole of his being was made up of a lifetime of moments, each bearing within them the failings and wanderings of his flesh. He knew he could be forgiven, but how could he become *new*?

Jesus went on to explain that the kingdom of God was one of spirit, not flesh. No flesh could ever, in and of itself, become fit for the kingdom.

Nicodemus remembered his frustration in that moment. *Then how? What hope was there?*

Outside the walls of the upper room, a powerful gust of wind rushed by, tossing debris, and rattling the rooftop in its wake. Jesus said, "*The wind blows wherever it pleases. You hear its sound, but you cannot tell where it comes from or where it is going. So it is with everyone born of the Spirit*" (John 3:8).

Nicodemus still had struggled to understand, but then Jesus explained to him that it was not a work of regeneration that he would accomplish on his own. It would be a work of grace, a gift received. As a teacher of the Law, Nicodemus knew Moses, so Jesus turned to the stories of Moses to explain. Jesus reminded Nicodemus of how God had instructed Moses to craft a bronze snake in the wilderness and put it on a pole so that when the children of Israel were bitten by poisonous snakes, they might look to the bronze snake and be healed. Nicodemus, of course, understood they were healed not by the snake itself but by their hope in the mercy of their Father in heaven. Jesus now explained the snake was more than a symbol of faith. It was foreshadowing of a greater redemption to come.

———

A second nail clinked to the ground, and Nicodemus turned his face up to the Man on the cross as the full weight of Jesus' next words fell upon him: *"Just as Moses lifted up the snake in the wilderness, so the Son of Man must be lifted up, that everyone who believes may have eternal life in him"* (John 3:14–15).

Tears flowed down Nicodemus's face as he understood at last how he would in fact be made new and able to enter the kingdom of God. It was never anything he would be able to accomplish on his own. It was an act of faith in a sacrifice freely given by One far greater than he. He had once recognized Jesus as a teacher from God. Now Nicodemus knew He had been so much more. Nicodemus and Joseph moved forward and raised their arms to receive the body of the Messiah, the Perfect Lamb of God, as the last nail fell from His wrist to the ground below.

The price had been paid, and Nicodemus, even though he was old, was born again.

Prayer

Perfect Lamb of God,

You are worthy of all praise. In You my sins like scarlet are made white as snow[1] and all my strivings cease. Morning by morning, I turn my eyes to You, resting in the hope of Your redemption. You are the Lover of my Soul, and I adore You.

Amen

1. Isaiah 1:18

"I Have Seen the Lord!"

Mary Magdalene

I keep my eyes always on the LORD.
With him at my right hand, I will not be shaken.
Therefore my heart is glad and my tongue rejoices;
my body also will rest secure,
because you will not abandon me to the realm of the dead,
nor will you let your faithful one see decay.
You make known to me the path of life;
you will fill me with joy in your presence,
with eternal pleasures at your right hand.

PSALM 16:8–11

MARY MAGDALENE SAT IN the pre-dawn stillness before the flickering light of an oil lamp. The door to her left stood slightly ajar so that she could watch the horizon for the first streaks of gray. Those first streaks would herald the end of the Sabbath and the dawn of a new day . . . the third day.

Tradition held that until the third day, the soul of the newly deceased hovered near the body and that it wasn't until it departed that decomposition began. Mary glanced at the still-black horizon and wondered if Jesus' soul lingered near the garden tomb. Her heart longed to go to Him before the dawn ushered in the new day and carried His spirit away, but the Sabbath forbade it.

And so she would wait for the dawn that not only freed her to go to the tomb, but also freed His soul to leave Earth's bounds. For the rabbis taught that God would never leave the just in anguish more than three days.

> "After two days he will revive us;
>   on the third day he will restore us,
>   that we may live in his presence."
> HOSEA 6:2

"My God . . ." Mary groaned, as she closed her eyes and tears began to run down her face. The cruel anguish Jesus endured on the cross still burned so vividly for her. She had witnessed every torturous strain against the nails, every gasp for breath, until He cried out and breathed His last. It not only seemed impossible that He was dead, but that He *could* die. How could He who had given sight to the blind and raised Lazarus from the dead be conquered by death? How could He who had broken through the nightmare of Mary's own torment and delivered her from the grasp of seven demons be nailed to a cross by mere men?

Blinking back the tears, she ran her fingers along the twine that secured the package of spices in her lap. Then, lifting her eyes again to check the horizon, she found it still cloaked with night. She turned her attention back to the package and lovingly smoothed the creases in the wrappings as more memories of that day pushed their way back into her mind.

Mary had waited near the cross until they took His body down. To her amazement, two Jewish leaders, men of wealth, came to claim it: Joseph of Arimathea and Nicodemus. She and some of the other women followed them to a nearby garden tomb and watched from a distance as these prominent men and their attendants carried the body inside. According to the burial tradition, the body would be first laid on a stone table in the center chamber of the tomb and washed with warm water. Afterward, those preparing the body for burial would wrap the torso and each limb separately, layering the strips with a mixture of aloe and myrrh. A separate linen cloth would be used to wrap the head. But on this day everything was done in haste because the Sabbath was quickly approaching. The women couldn't see how well the body was prepared from their vantage point, and they could not bear the thought that their Lord would be denied a proper burial. So, just as they had provided for His ministry out of their resources when He was living, they would now take the initiative to be sure He was honored in His death.

As soon as morning dawned, they would go to the tomb to offer Him the only expression of adoration left to them. They would anoint His body with the aloes and myrrh. The women would anoint the body with spices in an attempt to simply mask decomposition, but Mary knew it could do nothing to slow it. Death had won, and now nothing would slow its ruthless march through His body until all was consumed. Her offering of spices represented both the depth of her adoration for Jesus and the absolute devastation of her hope, but it was all she had to offer Him, so she and the other women would do what they could. Mary would go ahead of the others and arrange for the removal of the stone.

Mary lifted her eyes to the door once again and saw that at last the horizon was tinted with the first hints of gray. She took a deep breath, lifted the burial spices from her lap, and then rose to extinguish the lamp in its niche in the wall. It was time.

The bright moon above lit her way. Mary moved quickly and quietly through the deserted streets to the edge of the city. Her thoughts were focused on the task ahead, particularly the challenge of the stone. She hoped the gardener would perhaps have arrived for his morning duties and be willing to assist her. Soon, she exited the city gate and drew near the site of the crucifixion, Golgotha, the Place of the Skull. The metallic scent of blood still hung heavily in the air. Mary purposefully kept her eyes from the site and quickened her pace to cover the remaining distance to the garden.

When she arrived, she gratefully ducked beneath the graceful palms that flanked the entrance and then paused for a moment to catch her breath. Fig trees sweetly scented the air. The last rays of moonlight peeked through the thin, silvery leaves of the olive trees, and cast a gentle glow over the pink and white blooms of the almond trees. A heavy, serene silence blanketed the place. Mary took a deep breath, closed her eyes, and held the burial spices tightly to her chest, mingling their woodsy aroma with the sweetness of the garden. Her grief was as heavy as the stone that awaited her at the sepulcher door. Tears flowed down her cheeks as she slowly began to take the final few steps down the worn path.

A moment later, she rounded the bend and the tomb glowed white in the moonlight in front of her.

But there was a dark gaping hole in the tomb's center where the stone should have been.

Mary's heart began pounding, and a roaring sound filled her ears. She dropped the burial spices to the ground and reached out to steady herself against the trunk of a nearby palm.

Jesus was gone. There was no other reason for the removal of the stone. Someone had taken the body!

"No!" Mary cried. She doubled over and gasped for air. Then she stood and gazed in astonishment at the empty tomb for a moment longer before turning and running from the garden into the sleeping streets of Jerusalem. She had to tell Peter and John.

Soon she was frantically knocking on the door of the home where the men were staying. A wary reply came from behind the locked door.

"Who is there?"

"It is me, Mary. Quickly! Open the door!"

Mary heard the bolt slide in the lock. Then the heavy wooden door opened, and Peter and John ushered her inside. She looked into their anxious faces.

"They have taken the Lord out of the tomb, and we don't know where they have put him!" Mary said. (John 20:2)

Without a word the two men turned and ran from the house and in the direction of the garden tomb. Mary followed them into the street. She tried to keep up with them, but they were too fast for her. Soon, they were out of sight.

When she once again arrived at the garden, the sun had not quite risen. She was sure they were already at the tomb and hurried along the path to meet them. When she arrived at the grave, the two men had completed their inspection and were already walking away. The moonlight across their faces illuminated no answers, only bewilderment.

There was nothing more for Peter and John to do. They slowly turned and walked back toward the garden entrance. A moment later, she was left alone in the stillness once again.

As Mary stood before the gaping entrance of the tomb, a terrible torrent of grief engulfed her soul. She wrapped her arms around her waist, and turned her face to the sky as a deep, rending wail escaped her lips. Sobs shook her body as her knees gave way, and she fell face down in the dust. She wept until the ground beneath her was saturated with her tears.

Weak from exhaustion, she struggled to her feet. Then, just as the sky above her was lightening with the first hues of sunrise, Mary once again walked to the entrance of the tomb and bent down to look inside. In the dim light of the tomb she saw two men wearing white, sitting where Jesus' body had been. One was at the head of the burial niche, the other at the foot.

"Woman, why are you crying?" (John 20:13).

"They have taken my Lord away," Mary said, "and I don't know where they have put him."

Then she sensed someone standing behind her. She turned around to look just as the first rays of sunlight broke through the branches of the trees overhead. Mary squinted into the glare as a man, who she assumed was the gardener, addressed her.

"Woman, why are you crying? Who is it you are looking for?"

"Sir, if you have carried him away, tell me where you have put him, and I will get him" (John 20:15).

Mary's great love for Jesus convinced her in that moment that if she only knew where His body was, she could carry it to safety alone. Her grief overcame her again, and she turned away from the Man to weep against the wall of the tomb.

And then He called her name.

"*Mary.*"

Once, long ago, Jesus had called her name, breaking through the darkness of her oppression to set her free from the seven demons that bound her. Now He broke through the hopelessness of her grief and despair. Mary might not have recognized His face, but she could never forget the sound of His voice, not when He called her name.

"Rabboni!" Mary gasped, and threw herself at His feet. Mary laughed through her tears as the scent of myrrh and aloes drifted up to her and she realized the men must have anointed Him for burial after all, but their efforts had all been in vain, for the feet in her hands were warm, strong, alive.

Then Jesus gently spoke again, and there was a smile in His voice. "*Do not hold on to me, for I have not yet ascended to the Father. Go instead to my brothers and tell them, 'I am ascending to my Father and your Father, to my God and your God'*" (John 20:17).

Mary relinquished her Savior's feet and ran to obey His command. The streets of Jerusalem were flooded with morning light as she reached John's home. She pounded on the locked door, and when John opened it, she burst inside to find the room filled with the disciples. They turned to her with stunned and wary faces, fearful of what news she might bring.

But the news was miraculous and wonderful. The words of Hosea were true after all.

> *After two days he will revive us;*
> *on the third day he will restore us,*
> *that we may live in his presence.*
> HOSEA 6:2

Mary's face was dust and tear-streaked, but she beamed as she made her announcement. "I have seen the Lord!" (John 20:18).

Prayer

My Risen Savior,

There are times when the turmoil in my mind and heart blinds me to Your comfort and glory which are ever near. I am so thankful that the meagerness of my faith doesn't hinder Your nearness to me. You come to me in compassion, drawn by my love for You and need of You.

Let the light of Your morning break through the darkness of my grief, doubt, and despair. Whisper my name once again, my Savior, and still my soul.

Amen

EMMAUS

———

The Lord *upholds all who fall*
and lifts up all who are bowed down.
The eyes of all look to you,
and you give them their food at the proper time.
You open your hand
and satisfy the desires of every living thing.
The Lord *is righteous in all his ways*
and faithful in all he does.

Psalm 145:14–17

FOR THE DISCIPLES THE past three days had been a cauldron of swirling emotions, stress, and trauma. The men had seen their Rabbi betrayed and crucified. Then, on the third morning after Jesus' death, some of the women came to declare the mystery of His empty tomb. They said they had seen an angel who told them Jesus had risen from the dead, but when Peter and John went to investigate, there was no angel to be found. The body, however, was gone. The tomb contained nothing more than a pile of discarded grave clothes.

Two of the men, Cleopas and Luke,[1] were worn out with it all. They needed to escape the crowded, bloodstained city for a while.

The men left Jerusalem through the Western Gate and followed the smooth Roman road out of the city. The early afternoon sun warmed them as the space between the homes that lined the road lengthened. The air was fragrant with new life as flowers and trees answered spring's call.

After an hour of walking, the men entered a pleasant valley. A short time later, they left the Roman road and turned onto the road toward Emmaus. The path sloped gently upward as it rose out of the valley.

As Cleopas and Luke walked, they discussed all that had occurred over the last few days. There was so much to try to understand. They were sure Jesus had been God's Prophet, yet their leaders had crucified Him. Then to have the women say He was alive . . . It was difficult to know what to believe.

The two men crested the hill and saw in the distance the ridge that sheltered Emmaus. Another path intersected theirs, and a Stranger who had been traveling along the adjoining road fell into step beside them. He walked with them, listening quietly as they continued to sort through all that had happened. After a moment, He turned to them and smiled.

"What are you discussing together as you walk along?" He asked (Luke 24:17).

The men stopped abruptly. Cleopas and Luke looked at each other and then down at the ground. When they lifted their heads again to answer the Stranger, their faces were etched with sorrow.

"Are you the only one visiting Jerusalem who does not know the things that have happened there in these days?" Cleopas asked the Stranger (Luke 24:18).

"What things?" the Man asked (Luke 24:19).

"About Jesus of Nazareth," they replied. "He was a prophet, powerful in word and deed before God and all the people. The chief priests and our rulers handed him over to be sentenced to death, and they crucified him; but we had hoped that he was the one who was going to redeem Israel. And what is more, it is the third day since all this took place. In addition, some of our women amazed us. They went to the tomb early this morning but didn't find his body. They came and told us that they had seen a vision of angels, who said he was alive. Then some of our companions went to the tomb and found it just as the women had said, but they did not see Jesus" (Luke 24:19–24).

The Stranger placed a hand on Luke's shoulder and then motioned to them to walk with Him.

"How foolish you are, and how slow to believe all that the prophets have spoken!" He said. *"Did not the Messiah have to suffer these things and then enter into his glory?"* (Luke 24:25–26).

> *As they walked, the Stranger began to explain to them how everything that had happened to Jesus had been foretold in the Scriptures.*

He began with Moses and then explained the prophets as well.

Cleopas and Luke listened with expectant hearts. Each step they took with the Stranger on the road to Emmaus seemed to lighten the sorrow that had settled over them since three days earlier when Jesus had been crucified. Soon the remaining distance to Emmaus had been traversed. The sun was low in the sky as the Stranger bid them good-bye and turned to continue down the road.

"Wait!" Luke said. "It is getting dark. Don't travel any farther tonight, Friend."

"Yes, please," Cleopas continued. "Come stay with us and continue Your journey tomorrow."

The Stranger agreed. Soon the men were gathered around a table for the evening meal. Soft lamplight flickered over fresh bread, broiled fish, and goblets filled with fragrant wine.

The Stranger took the bread and thanked God for it. He broke a piece from the loaf and smiled as He handed it to Cleopas.

Suddenly, it was as if a veil was lifted from the disciples' eyes. They gasped in recognition. It was Jesus!

Then He simply . . . disappeared.

Cleopas and Luke sat staring at the place where He had been. The bread, freshly broken, lay on the table. Luke turned to Cleopas.

"Were not our hearts burning within us while he talked with us on the road and opened the Scriptures to us?" he asked (Luke 24:32).

Cleopas nodded. "We have to go back to Jerusalem to tell the others," he said.

Luke agreed, and the two men rose, leaving their dinner uneaten on the table. When they stepped back onto the Emmaus Road, they relied on the bright spring moon to illuminate their path.

It had been a very long day, but they hardly noticed the seven-mile walk. Their hearts, which only a few hours before had been weighted down with grief, were now filled with joy. The cross and the horrors of the grave had been transformed by the power of a risen Messiah who had broken bread with them at the table, the Bread of Life Himself who had joined them as they walked along the road to Emmaus.

Prayer ———————————————————————————

My Risen Savior,

   How many times have I been blind to Your presence as You journeyed with me on the road of my loss? How often have You whispered meaning and purpose to me as we walked along the way to find I only have ears for the voice of my unbelief?

   Break the Bread of Life for me once again, Messiah, that I might know You. Your words are life and power. May my heart burn for You alone.

Amen

1. Scripture does not name the second man, but many authorities believe it to have been Luke. His account of the Emmaus encounter with Christ is especially vivid. It is possible that the very fact the second man remains unnamed is an additional indication Luke was the second man. This follows the pattern of John choosing to frequently omit his own name in his gospel account calling himself "the one Jesus loved."

Thomas's
Doubt

I remember the days of long ago;
*   I meditate on all your works*
*   and consider what your hands have done.*
I spread out my hands to you;
*   I thirst for you like a parched land.*
Answer me quickly, LORD;
*   my spirit fails.*
Do not hide your face from me
*   or I will be like those who go down to the pit.*
Let the morning bring me word of your unfailing love,
*   for I have put my trust in you.*

PSALM 143:5–8

Thomas burst into his home as evening shadows fell across the threshold. He quickly shut the door behind him and began to sob. Sweat beaded along the back of his hand as he struggled to secure the lock with trembling fingers. After several attempts, the bolt slid into place at last.

He turned to lean against the door and slowly slid to the floor. Jesus, Thomas's Rabbi, his Messiah, was gone. The world had turned upside down in a flurry of betrayal and injustice until Golgotha lay awash in the blood of his Friend. Jesus had been tortured to death, nailed to a Roman cross.

Thomas moaned and then stood to his feet. He climbed the short flight of stairs that led to the main room of his small home. He began moving each chair and bench against the wall where he turned them upside down, the tradition mandated for a home in mourning. When he was finished, he sat down on the floor, placed his forehead on his knees, and wept as the room grew dark and night fell.

Thomas spent two more days in solitude. His only companions were the shifting shadows that marked the passing hours and the horrific images of Jesus' wounds that tormented his dreams. The other disciples had drawn together, seeking the comfort of one another's company. He knew he was welcome to join them, but it was his nature to seek quiet while he waited for some measure of calm to return to his soul.

As the moments stretched into hours and then days, Thomas kept vigil for his Friend as he poured out his grief to God alone. The third day rose and passed as the previous two in quiet remembrance, desperate weeping, and the futile struggle to understand such devastating loss.

Then, the silence was shattered.

Loud fists fell on his door as shouts rang out in the night. "Thomas, Thomas! Open the door. It is us!"

He rushed to the door in response to the familiar voices of Peter, James, John, and the others. The moment he slid the lock open, the men filled the entry hall.

John stepped forward and pulled Thomas into an embrace before passing him off to James. He too pulled him near, and then held him at arms' length as he beamed into Thomas's bewildered face.

"Thomas, we have just seen the Lord. He lives!" he said.

Thomas felt his face flush as a roaring filled his ears and his vision began to dim. He stumbled backward and sat down on the stairs directly behind him. He leaned forward for a moment and took a few deep breaths to calm himself as the crowd of men quieted in front of him.

Could it possibly be true? But I saw the wounds . . .

Thomas stood, braced his right hand against the wall, and then climbed the stairs as the men followed. He took a few halting steps forward and sat down on the floor. His friends filed into the room and walked to the wall to turn the benches and chairs upright before taking their seats.

The room grew quiet as everyone waited for Thomas's response. After a moment, he turned to them. "I don't understand. What are you saying?" he stammered.

John began. "It has been an eventful day, friend. This morning, Mary Magdalene came to us and told us she had been to the tomb and that Jesus' body was gone. Peter and I ran to the garden to see for ourselves. We found the tomb empty. The body was missing, but the grave clothes had been left behind. We didn't know what to think. Mary Magdalene stayed behind at the tomb after we left. A while later she came to us once again, this time saying she had seen the Lord after our departure from the garden. She said He was alive!"

Luke joined in next. "Later in the day, Cleopas and I were walking to Emmaus when we were joined by Someone we at first thought was a stranger. As we walked, He began explaining how the prophets had fore-told all that would happen to Jesus. We were absolutely captivated! When we arrived at home, we asked Him to stay for dinner, and He agreed. When we sat down to eat, He took the bread, gave thanks, and broke it. Suddenly, our eyes were opened. It was Him—Jesus! And then He was gone. He simply disappeared. Of course, we rushed back to Jerusalem to tell the others."

Peter continued the narrative. "We were all gathered together with the doors locked, for fear of what the Pharisees might do next," he said. "Suddenly Jesus was standing right there in the room with us. He said, 'Peace be with you' (Luke 24:36). We were terrified, I tell you. We thought it was a ghost. He said, *'Why are you troubled, and why do doubts rise in your minds?'*" (Luke 24:38).

Peter shook his head, and when he continued, his voice was quieter. "Then He held out His arm to us and lifted the sleeve of His robe to show us the scar left behind where they nailed Him to the cross."

Thomas's eyes filled with tears as Peter finished speaking. He so desperately wanted it to be true.

He was a man of facts and measures. He was willing to die for what he knew, but how could he reconcile the horrors of the cross with this proclamation of life?

In Thomas's absence, Jesus had shown Himself to the other men and allowed them to touch Him. He wanted the same proof. His broken heart couldn't risk so precious a hope only to find it was a misunderstanding or illusion.

He looked at his friends and then quietly spoke. "Unless I see the nail marks in his hands and put my finger where the nails were, and put my hand into his side, I will not believe" (John 20:25).

An awkward silence settled over the room as the men looked at each other uncomfortably. John took a deep breath and knelt before Thomas. He placed a hand on his shoulder and said, "I am sure you will get that chance very soon, friend. Now, please, come with us. It is not good for you to stay here alone any longer."

Thomas nodded and stood as his friends rose to leave. When he reached the entrance of his home, he paused for a moment and took a final look back before extinguishing the oil lamp that rested in its niche in the wall. Then he closed the door behind him and followed the other men into the night.

A long week of waiting passed. The men prayed and shared hopes of what was to come, but as each new evening fell with no additional appearance of Jesus, Thomas grew anxious and impatient. On the morning of the eighth day, he stood at the window watching a steady stream of pilgrims prepare to leave Jerusalem and return home at the conclusion of the feasts. He sighed in frustration. It was time for them to begin their journey to Galilee, and still there was no sign of Jesus. He walked over to the closed door and placed his hand on the threshold before leaning his forehead against the rough wood.

If Jesus is really alive, why has He not shown Himself?

Suddenly there was a chorus of exclamation behind him.

Thomas turned to see Jesus standing in the middle of the room!

As the other disciples gathered excitedly around Him, He smiled at them.

"Peace be with you!" He said (John 20:26).

Jesus turned to look across the room at Thomas. His smile softened. He held His arm out to Thomas as He rolled up the sleeve of His robe to expose a dark red scar. He took a few steps toward Thomas, and when He spoke, His voice was filled with compassion.

"Put your finger here; see my hands. Reach out your hand and put it into my side. Stop doubting and believe" (John 20:27).

A sob caught in Thomas' throat. Jesus had just used the very words he himself had spoken a week before. Jesus had been there all along . . .

Thomas found he no longer needed the test he had proposed. As he gazed at the risen Savior, all doubt faded away. In fact, he saw with a faith more vibrant and clear than his brothers. Thomas took a step nearer to Jesus and fell at His feet. At that moment the one who was last to believe became the first to proclaim the risen Christ's divinity.

"My Lord and my God!" (John 20:28).

Prayer ───────────────────────────

My Risen Savior,

Even when I am broken by sorrow and crippled by doubt, You receive me with tender compassion. I am so glad You know and understand me completely . . . and yet love me anyway. Help me know You are near even when my path is uncertain, and my faith worn thin. Then restore my strength once again that I might glorify Your name.

Amen

THE RESTORATION OF PETER

Create in me a pure heart, O God,
*   and renew a steadfast spirit within me.*
Do not cast me from your presence
*   or take your Holy Spirit from me.*
Restore to me the joy of your salvation
*   and grant me a willing spirit, to sustain me.*

PSALM 51:10–12

BEFORE YOU BEGIN, READ JOHN 21:1–19

"I'M GOING FISHING," PETER announced.

"We will go with you," his friends responded.

The seven of them gathered their equipment and walked to the shore of the Sea of Galilee where a steady breeze tossed an endless procession of low waves gently onto the sand. Peter shrugged the net from his shoulder and into the boat as he thoughtfully ran one hand along the soft, weathered wood of the prow of their thirty-foot vessel. The deep cerulean sky above him faded into shades of rose before swelling into a crescendo of scarlet along the horizon as the sun dipped below the hill line in the distance. Night was falling. The moon was rising. The life of a Galilean fisherman was calling.

As the moon rose over the surface of the water, they pushed off from shore, guiding their boat into the deep. Peter took off his outer robe to free his arms for the labors ahead and then reached down to grasp a trammel net with experienced hands. The others joined him, and they threw the net into the moonlight. It hovered for an instant before breaking the surface of the water with a splash. Peter watched as it sank below the surface. Then he settled down to wait.

The other men in the boat chatted quietly for a while about Jesus' crucifixion and miraculous resurrection. He had appeared to them twice. There was no doubting it; He was alive again. But Peter, once so boisterous, was quiet now despite the joyous return of Jesus. He was weighted down by regret. He had denied and abandoned his friend when He needed his support most. How could Jesus ever forgive him or trust him in the future?

Peter rose to grasp the edges of the net and haul it from the water. There wasn't a single fish. Again, the net was thrown and the wait began. As the night stretched long, conversation in the boat gave way to the rhythm of the net breaking the moonlit surface of the water only to be drawn back empty time and again.

Nothing. But so much time to think.

Peter couldn't help but remember another fishless night years before when Jesus simply spoke the word from shore and filled his nets. Then Jesus had changed his life.

"Don't be afraid; from now on you will fish for people," Jesus had said (Luke 5:10).

Something in His call stirred Peter. He knew he had found his true purpose. He left everything—his father's trade, his boat, his nets. He abandoned all to follow Jesus and seek the kingdom of God. He had seen unspeakable wonders . . . The blind saw. The lame leaped. Jesus calmed the wind and waves by just speaking a word. Peter had come to believe Jesus was more than a prophet. He was the Messiah.

Peter had even seen Jesus transfigured in all His glory. Moses and Elijah came from heaven to speak with Him before Peter's very eyes! Later, he had pledged his allegiance to Jesus. He promised to follow Him even to prison and death.

Oh, how Peter believed! Oh, how he *loved* this Rabbi from Nazareth. But when the moment of testing came, his belief and love weren't enough to stand in the face of his fear. He had crumbled; and in the high priest's courtyard, he had denied his Messiah, his *closest Friend,* three times. How could Jesus forgive him when he couldn't even forgive himself?

Shaking his head to clear away the memories, he rose to pull the net from the water. It broke the surface just as the first rays of sunrise began to paint the edge of the horizon in gold, pink, and red. The net was empty.

Much like Peter's broken heart.

"Friends," a voice called out, breaking the silence of the cool gray shadows of the beach. "Haven't you any fish?" (John 21:5).

"No . . ."

"Throw your net on the right side of the boat and you will find some," He called back.

Peter's heart beat a little faster. *Could it be?*

Once more, the net hovered over the surface of the water, and then splashed down into it, scattering ribbons of red and gold. Peter took a deep breath and then joined his friends in grasping the edges of the net. Calloused fingers gripped tightly and lifted upward. It was so heavy, too heavy to lift . . .

John leaned down next to him and whispered in his ear, "It is the Lord!"

> *Though Peter was broken by failure, his love for Jesus remained strong.*

He couldn't wait for the boat to make it to shore. Peter grabbed his robe, wrapped it around him, and leaped into the water to make his way to Jesus. He half swam, half ran to the beach. Once ashore, he walked to Jesus as water dripped from his robe, hair, and beard. When Peter reached Him, what he found stunned him. Jesus had made breakfast. Peter did not miss the significance. In his culture, a meal was never just a meal; it was a symbol. In preparing food and inviting him to partake, Jesus was powerfully affirming His acceptance of Peter. He was telling Peter in the most tangible way possible that all was forgiven.

Peter stood silently before the scene, taking it in. Jesus looked up at his friend and smiled. Then He nodded toward the other disciples who were making their way onto shore with the catch. Quietly He said, *"Bring some of the fish you have just caught"* (John 21:10).

Peter's eyes filled with tears as he nodded before going to his friends. He ran to the boat, grasped the edges of the heavy net and helped haul it onto the beach. Then he reached inside, grasped a fish in each hand, and followed his friends back to the fire.

They breakfasted on warm fish and bread. Good conversation flowed around the fire, but Peter was still quiet. He still struggled to make peace with his failure in spite of the fact Jesus had demonstrated His acceptance and forgiveness. A deeper work of restoration and healing was needed.

Later, Jesus would undertake the painful work as the two of them walked along the beach. Jesus motioned back to the others still lingering by the fire, and gently reminded Peter of his boast that even if they all turned away, he would not. *"Simon, son of John, do you love me more than these?"*

But Peter was past boasting or comparing himself to anyone else. He had learned just how weak he really was. Only one thing was still sure. He did, indeed, love Jesus.

He stared out at the water and, in pain, replied, "Yes, Lord, you know that I love you."

Then Jesus called him once again to his purpose. He had once asked Peter to fish for men, but this time He asked his friend to care for those new citizens of the kingdom of God with the most humble of illustrations: *"Feed my lambs"* (John 21:15).

Jesus had described Himself as "The Good Shepherd" who cared for His sheep. He was asking Peter to join Him in this ministry.

A few more steps . . . and another question.

"Simon, son of John, do you love me?"

"Yes, Lord, you know that I love you."

"Take care of my sheep" (John 21:16).

But there were three denials that haunted Peter's quietest moments, and three denials were in need of restoration. A third question followed the second.

"Simon, son of John, do you love me?"

Peter winced and his face reddened. His voice broke with his response. "Lord, You know all things; You know that I love You."

Jesus stopped walking and looked long at Peter before calling him to his purpose one final time.

"Feed my sheep. Very truly I tell you, when you were younger you dressed yourself and went where you wanted; but when you are old you will stretch out

your hands, and someone else will dress you and lead you where you do not want to go" (John 21:17–18).

Peter bowed his head as he absorbed the prophecy of his future. It was one of both horror and redemption. He would follow his Messiah to the inexpressible suffering of his own Roman cross. It was a death brutal enough to chill the heart of any man. The promise wrapped inside the darkness was that Peter *would,* by God's grace, ultimately be faithful where once before he had failed so miserably. Where his own love and loyalty had failed him, God's strength would lead him.

Jesus placed a firm hand on Peter's shoulder. He had one final call for this broken one, now restored by grace.

"Follow me!" (John 21:19).

Prayer

Merciful Savior,

I come to You broken by my failure and helpless in my need. Pretense is lost. Pride abandoned.

But You, tender Christ, mend the broken. And though the process of my restoration is painful at times for me, it is one You are forever faithful to undertake with meticulous loving care. You understand my heart when my heart is a mystery to me. You heal me when I cannot even comprehend my wounds.

You restore my soul, and I worship You.

Amen

GLOSSARY

---

amphora(e): an ancient jar used to hold oil or wine

basalt: a dense, dark grey stone formed from solidified lava

Bashan: a rich, fertile area in northern Israel, now known as the Golan Heights

Bethphage: "house of unripe figs"; the city limits of Jerusalem at the time of Christ

Caesarea Maritima: an ancient, Roman-style city, built by Herod the Great on Israel's Mediterranean coast

Caves of Arbela: caves in the cliffs overlooking ancient Capernaum where Jewish Zealots, along with their families, were slaughtered by Herod the Great

cock crow: the trumpet blast that announced the start of the liturgical day. (According to Rabbinic law, it was actually forbidden to keep chickens in Jerusalem.)

Court of the Gentiles: the large, outer court of the Temple. No Gentile was allowed beyond this court.

Court of Women: the Temple court just beyond the Court of the Gentiles. No woman was allowed to go beyond this court. It was also called the Court of the Treasury because monetary offerings were received there.

Decapolis: Greco-Roman cities east of the Sea of Galilee

Decumanus Maximus: the main street in a Roman town

denarii: an ancient Roman coin

Feast of Tabernacles: a feast to remember the forty years Israel lived in tents in the desert; also known as Sukkot

Feast of Unleavened Bread: feast to remember the haste with which the Israelites left Egypt. (During their exodus, there was no time for the bread to rise.)

Gabbai: a common tax collector

Gabbatha, the Stone Pavement: "the knoll, or raised place"; the place where Roman authorities pronounced judgment

Hasmonaean: a family of Jewish patriots who ruled Israel from 142–63 BC; also known as the Maccabees

Hercules: a Greek/Roman demigod famous for his strength

Herod's winter palace (Jericho): an opulent palace built in Jericho by Herod the Great on the site of a former Hasmonaean palace

Herodium: a conical shaped fortress-palace built by Herod the Great

International Highway: major ancient trade route in Israel

John Hyrcanus (Herod the Great's puppet high priest): the high priest appointed by Herod the Great. He was considered to be disloyal to his own people, an instrument of Herod and Rome.

Joy of the Feast: the ceremonial lighting of the large candelabras in the Court of Women on the first night of the Feast of the Tabernacles

Kidron Valley: a valley to the north and east of Jerusalem that separates the city from the Mount of Olives

Maccabean palace: the residence of the Hasmonaean rulers in Jerusalem. It was located on the western side of the Upper City. It is also known as the Hasmonaean palace.

Masada: Herod the Great's fortress palace built in the desert. Long after his death, Jewish Zealots committed suicide at Masada rather than surrender to the Romans. It is a symbol of Jewish nationalism.

Matthais Antigonus: the last of the Hasmonean/Maccabean line to rule Israel. He was assassinated by Herod the Great.

mikveh: ceremonial purification bath

Mokhes: tax-collector, a customhouse official

Mount of Olives: the hills which provide the eastern border of Jerusalem

murex: sea snail from which dye for cloth was made

Gates of Nicanor/Nicanor Gates: one of the gates on the east side of the Temple which led into the courtyard

observant Judaism: Jews who are faithful to God's law as given through Moses

opobalsamum: a small tree from which a resin was extracted that was believed to cure a variety of illnesses. It is also known as the "Balm of Gilead".

Paschal: Passover

Phasael, Mariamme, and Hippicus (Herod the Great's lofty towers): the three towers of Herod the Great's citadel in Jerusalem. They are named after his brother, favorite wife, and best friend.

Pool of Israel: a pool dug by Herod the Great in Jerusalem as part of the Temple expansion project

porticoes of the Pool of Bethesda: the porches surrounding the Pool of Bethesda where the diseased and lame would rest while waiting and hoping for healing

Psalms of Ascent: Psalms 120–134. Also known as the Songs of Degrees.

Roman pools of Asclepius: Roman pools dedicated to the worship of Asclepius, the god of healing. These Roman pools were located near the Jewish Pool of Bethesda.

sedile: a wooden block seat on the cross

Servant Songs of Isaiah: four passages of scripture of similar form found in Isaiah that are Messianic in nature—Isaiah 42:1–4, Isaiah 49:1–6, Isaiah 50:4–10, Isaiah 52:13–53:12

shekhinah glory: the visible manifestation of God

shofar: a trumpet made from a ram's horn

shofarot: collection boxes in the Court of Women/Court of Treasury that had a "shofar" shaped metal tube at the top. Coins were dropped in this tube, which then fell into the box below it.

sluice gates: a wooden or metal barrier that slides in grooves to allow an operator to control flow in a waterway

Teachers of the Law: the rabbis, scribes, and Pharisees dedicated to the study, and interpretation of, the Mosaic law.

Temple of Zeus: a temple of white marble built at Caesarea Philippi by Herod the Great in honor of Caesar Augustus

triclinium table: a low, three sided table; diners reclined at triclinium tables while eating

twenty-four courses: from the time of Moses, the priesthood was divided into twenty-four courses. The duties of the priesthood rotated between these priestly divisions.